A

MODERN GUIDE

FOR THE

PERPLEXED

A

MODERN GUIDE

FOR THE

PERPLEXED

By Leon I. Sones, M.D.

SPENSER PUBLISHING HOUSE

Copyright © 2021 by Leon I. Sones, M.D.

Spenser Publishing House, LLC
11661 San Vicente Boulevard, Suite 220
Los Angeles, CA 90049
www.spenserpublishinghouse.com

ISBN 978-1-7346130-9-4 (hardcover)
ISBN 978-1-7360377-0-6 (paperback)
ISBN 978-1-7360377-1-3 (e-book)

Cover and book design by Lisa Ham at spaceechoes.com
Cover Painting by Alexis Sones

A NOTE ABOUT THE TITLE

For those familiar with Maimonides's twelfth-century masterwork, *The Guide for the Perplexed*, it probably will seem very presumptuous of me to use the title I have chosen. However, I couldn't come up with a better title, and this book, if successful, may serve to activate an interest in Maimonides and his long-enduring legacy. Given that possibility, were he still alive, Maimonides might forgive my clearly flagrant, but flattering, plagiarism.

ON TAKING ADVICE FROM ME
OR ANYONE ELSE

Whenever I offer advice to patients, I invariably add this caveat (a caveat that also pertains to all the advice in this book):"I take no responsibility whatsoever for what you do with my advice."

My patients frequently kid me about the caveat: "Oh, here we go again with your disclaimer. You're just trying to protect yourself." My response is usually, "No. It's for your protection. Life is too complicated. I hear about what you are experiencing for forty-five minutes; you are living what you are describing and know a great deal more about it than I do. You have to hang in with your own good head. You can't go blindly with me or anybody else, including doctors, lawyers, or other 'experts.' If you deem the advice appropriate, use it; if it's not, discard it. It's you who have the responsibility for, and bear the consequences of, your actions."

SPECIAL ACKNOWLEDGEMENTS

My grandson, Josh, has been of enormous help in editing this book and putting it into digital format. He has put his training in computer science at Cornell University to very helpful use, and I am very grateful for his help.

I am also very grateful for my granddaughter, Alexis, who created the cover artwork for this book. Close examination of the cover will show that it artistically represents the state of being "perplexed." Alexis has been a wonderful painter since she was a child, and I am very proud to display her talent to all my readers.

INTRODUCTION

It may be of some interest to the reader to know something about me. If you look in the Brookline (Massachusetts) High School Yearbook for 1945, you will find my name, and under "Ambition," "To become a psychiatrist." Following discharge as a Technical Sergeant from the U.S. Army in 1948, I took pre-med courses at UCLA and after three years was admitted to the Medical School at the University of California in San Francisco. After an internship at Harbor General Hospital in Torrance, California, I began training in psychiatry at the UCLA School of Medicine, Department of Psychiatry. A critically important aspect of my training was my personal analysis with Norman A. Levy, M.D. Ever since 1959 I have been in the private practice of psychiatry, but with some additional experiences that are mentioned in some of the essays in this book and are also reflected in the following list of credentials:

- Diplomate, American Board of Psychiatry and Neurology
- Honorary Status, Assistant Clinical Professor, UCLA School of Medicine, Department of Psychiatry
- Emeritus, Attending Staff, Department of Psychiatry, Cedars-Sinai Medical Center
- Formerly, Attending Chief, Department of Psychiatry, Cedars-Sinai Medical Center
- Formerly, Founding Director, Consultation and Liaison Service, Cedars-Sinai Medical Center
- Formerly, Founding Chairman, Peer Review Committee, Department of Psychiatry, Cedars-Sinai Medical Center

Some words about my family are definitely in order, as they have reviewed and commented on virtually everything I have written. No words are enough to express the importance of the contribution to these essays (and my life in all its aspects) of my talented psychologist wife of sixty-six years, Dr. Gittelle K. Sones.

Significant contributions also have been made by my three physician sons and their families: Aaron, his wife Julie, and their children, Alexis and Harrison; Daniel, his wife Anna, and their children, Amy and Alex; and David, his wife Patti, and their children, Michael, Eli, and Joshua.

I have been writing this series of essays over the last several years. Usually the writing occurred after a session that especially illustrated an important problem. One consequence of writing in this fashion is that there may be a certain amount of repetition. That repetition usually is associated with something I consider particularly important.

The essays are not arranged in any special order, except for the first one, which I consider most important.

Finally, this book would obviously not be possible without the, by now, thousands of patients that opened their hearts and minds to me. My gratitude toward them is boundless. They validated that the eighteen-year-old high school graduate I was seventy-one years ago was on the right track when he wrote, "Ambition: To be a psychiatrist."

I hope you find something in these essays that can be helpful.

TABLE OF CONTENTS

1. Reality and Fantasy 1

2. Some Notes About Psychotherapy 11

3. Training Attention 17

4. Is That Physical Complaint Psychosomatic? 19

5. Social Anxiety Disorder 21

6. Emotion, Responsibility, and Verbal Abuse 23

7. In Psychotherapy, Talk About What You Are Reluctant to Talk
   About...25

8. If What You Are Doing Isn't Working, Try Something Else 27

9. Irrational Guilt and Unwanted Feelings 29

10. The Problem of Diagnosis in Psychiatry 31

11. Resignation 33

12. Chronic Lateness and Self-Discipline 35

13. Obsessive Compulsive Disorder 39

14. Run a Business or Do Social Service 41

15. On Proper Conduct of Extra-Marital Relationships 43

16. Feelings of Inferiority 45

17. Guilt in Ending a Relationship and Self-Esteem Problems.......47

18. Follow Your Bliss but Be Practical 49

19. The Mystery of Very Prolonged Distressing Reactions When
    Mates Discover Their Partner's Extra-Marital Affair 51

20. Marriage Versus Living Together 55

21. Examples of Appropriately Dealing With Youngsters 57*

22. Appropriate Role of Parents in Dealing With Their Adult
    Children 59

23. On Death 61

24. On Control of Feelings 63

25. Some Sound Advice in Dealing With Very Ill or Dying Patients..65

26. Psychotherapeutic Treatment of Psychotic Reactions 67

*Chapter written by Gittelle K. Sones, Ph.D., Ed.D.

27. Anger 69

28. On Lying 71

29. The Self-Esteem System 73

30. The Tendency to Generalize About Complex Human Beings ..77

31. Key to a Happy Marriage 79

32. Deprived of the Motivation of Money 81

33. Develop a Business of Your Own 83

34. Proper Conduct of Marital (or Non-Marital) Squabbling 85

35. Identification With a Disturbed Parent 87

36. How to Make a Woman Happy 89

37. Unwanted Neglected Children 91

38. Adrift With No Clear Vocational Path 93

39. Turn Adversity Into Advantage 95

40. Adolescent Rebellion 97

41. Potential Unfulfilled 99

42. What to Do If He Won't Commit 101

43. Online Dating 103

44. Usefulness of Negative Fantasy 105

45. Problem of Reading Other People's Minds 107

46. What Is the Meaning of Life? 109

47. Doing Psychotherapy 111

48. War 117

49. Final Essay 119

I. REALITY AND FANTASY

Henry David Thoreau: "The mass of men live lives of quiet desperation."

Many years ago, a young psychiatrist-in-training consulted me. He told me that one weekend while psychiatrist-on-call for his training hospital, he used his master keys to open the hospital library. He loved books and here he was -- alone in the library with an enormous number of books at his fingertips. He was also enamored of the concept of evolution and, while there alone in the library for many hours, he focused his reading on evolution. While doing so he began to have a series of fantasies about evolution's role in human psychology. He became extremely stimulated and had trouble sleeping. His difficulty sleeping and his stimulation mounted over the next several days and developed into a classic manic reaction. He had fantasies of a union with God, thought he was getting messages from the television, etc. During his consequent hospitalization, he had fantasies of struggling with a Communist Goliath (the Cold War with the Soviet Union was going on at the time). As part of that struggle, by throwing himself against it repeatedly, he actually broke down the reinforced locked door of the room in which he was placed and walked out in a blaze of glory. He might not have defeated the Russian, but that ended attempts to put him in a locked room.

After about ten days he urged his wife to take him out of the hospital. She, clearly having a great deal of confidence in him, took him home against medical advice. After about another ten days the manic reaction completely resolved. He was interviewed by a highly experienced and empathic psychiatrist on the training hospital staff, who, after cautioning him about further "flights of fantasy," okayed his return to the training program, provided he got into therapy. He had already begun therapy with me.

It should be noted that what I am describing in this essay all took place before we had any drugs for manic reactions. We currently have a number of such drugs, but during the period described herein, lithium, the first of these drugs, had not yet been used in manic states. Like virtually all psychological problems, the treatment was psychotherapy.

Despite apparent progress in therapy, he experienced another manic attack after his hospital training was complete and he was engaged in the private practice of psychiatry. It occurred after he was accepted for psychoanalytic training. At the time, psychoanalysis was the premier psychiatric treatment, and that he finally got accepted, despite his clear history of mania, was extremely stimulating. The pattern of subsequent symptoms was very similar to his first attack. He was once again hospitalized. He deeply disliked the hospital psychiatrist assigned to treat him and refused to talk to him. Further, he was enraged because his wife was not permitted to visit. In addition, while being forcibly held down, he was injected with Thorazine, a drug that he hated because it clouded his thinking. He desperately wanted to escape from his enforced hospitalization.

The psychiatric unit had a major security defect in that an elevator used by the rest of the hospital opened directly onto the psychiatric unit. My patient dressed up in typical doctor-type clothes and entered the elevator when it opened on the unit. With a rapidly beating heart he made his way out of the hospital and to the nearby home of his in-laws. His nurturing mother-in-law welcomed him. After a week or so at his in-laws', he was free of symptoms and returned to home and practice.

However, when the Psychoanalytic Institute became aware of this second attack, he was asked to resign from the Institute. He did so, but this was extremely painful, as becoming a psychoanalyst had been a goal of his ever since high school. It took a while for him to recover from this painful loss, but recover he did. That recovery was probably assisted to some degree by his recognition that the Institute represented, to a degree, a cohesive family -- something he had lost at about the same time he had decided he wanted to be a psychoanalyst.

In therapy, among many other things, we explored in some detail his omnipotent longings as they clearly came through in his manic states in the form of his fantasies of a direct connection with God, etc. My theory was that if he became aware of those longings, he would not be subject to finding their expression in manic states. It is possible that the work on his omnipotent longings played a role in the drama of what subsequently occurred, but they were clearly not the critical element.

Many months later he came into my office bitterly weeping. He told me that while driving to my office he happened to listen to some very stimulating classical music and began, once again, to fantasy that God was communicating with him. But at this point he began to weep and very firmly told himself that he was not going there. His manic episodes had resulted in the loss of psychoanalytic training, and had disrupted his family and his life in general. He had clearly, and for the first time, aborted a manic attack.

In subsequent therapy sessions, he explored in great detail how he had been able to stop the attack. He came to the conclusion that it was his recognition of the flow of manic fantasies that permitted him to abort the reaction. There was a part of his brain, probably in his frontal lobes, that stood apart from the flow of manic fantasies and their attendant intense emotion, and was able to block the manic attack. Certainly the pain he experienced consequent to the loss of the Institute enormously motivated that recognition.

In analytic work he did, quite independent of me, he came to the conclusion that the crucial task was to be acutely aware of when he was involved in fantasy. In order to do this, he decided that he needed a very clear definition of reality. The definition he established was, "Reality is the ongoing sensory field; that is, what I can see, hear, touch, smell, and taste at this moment in time and place. All else (with some few exceptions that are irrelevant for this discussion) is fantasy; that is, it is going on inside my head." He was very strict about this definition. He pointed to a picture that was in my line of vision and said, "That picture is reality for you, fantasy for me. Now I turn and look and it becomes reality for me. All fantasies have odds that they will become reality. The odds that when I turn and look that picture will be there are 99.9999..., continuing on indefinitely. It could, in some science-fiction fashion, disappear, but obviously the odds are enormously against that happening."

He, for a variety of reasons, elected not to write about this himself. He has given me his complete permission to do so. Further, I have elaborated on his definition in a variety of ways, as you will see below, that are independent of him. (He stopped therapy with me a long time ago though we do continue to communicate with one another.) He clearly convinced me of the psychotherapeutic value of this definition. I want to emphasize that this is neither a scientific nor a philosophical definition of reality. It is a psychotherapeutic definition, which you might find useful or not.

Interestingly, though most of my patients agree with the definition, the fact is that relatively few of them are able to use the definition in the way I recommend. Those few that do use it in the manner I suggest invariably say that it is the most important thing they've learned in therapy, and I obviously agree. Why the vast majority have such difficulty mystifies me. The force of habit is clearly involved. Beyond habit, and I suspect much more powerful, is that in implementing the definition described we are moving against deeply programmed evolutionary tendencies (see below). In addition, acceptance of the definition frequently leads to questioning nearly everything, including fundamental fantasies like, for example, one's belief in God. Further, it may be a heavy blow to self-esteem to acknowledge one's notion of "reality" has been wrong lifelong.

Now I am not preoccupied with whether my house will still be there when I drive home from work. Though if you understand the definition, it is clearly a fantasy that my house will be there. It is when experiencing emotional distress that the definition is ideally brought to bear. The question always is, are we reacting to reality or fantasy? The fact is that most suffering is due to fantasy. This is not to say that real suffering does not play an important role in life. Certainly, for example, the death of a child is an enormously painful event. But most suffering, at least what I see in my office, is not reality based. And I do not believe my patients differ from the population in general.

Examples of non-reality-based suffering -- that is, emotional reactivity to low-probability negative fantasies -- are ubiquitous: "I will never find a job I like." "She said the chemistry is not there. There must be something wrong with me. Nobody will ever love me." "There is no point in taking this exam. I know I won't pass." "If I don't follow this ritual, bad things will happen." "When I die, I know I will be all alone, adrift in a boundless, endless void."

Death by fantasy is not uncommon. It particularly occurs in patients suffering from Major Depression. I know of no other state, including far-advanced cancer, where, uniformly, patients all have thoughts of suicide. They inevitably fantasy, "There's no point in going on. This misery is endless. I might as well kill myself." I call it "death by fantasy" because with appropriate treatment virtually every such patient will recover completely.

We see the tendency to negatively fantasy played out on national and international levels: "The Vietnamese are involved in a vast monolithic Communist conspiracy to take over the world. We must go to war to stop them." "Saddam Hussein has weapons of mass destruction. We must go into Iraq and destroy them." The tragic consequences of these fantasies are spelled out in enormous amounts of blood and treasure.

Some evidence supporting the theory that we humans have a marked tendency to get involved in negative fantasy is provided by a study conducted at Harvard and reported by John Tierney in the *New York Times*, November 15, 2010. Psychologists randomly called people all over the world and asked them what they were doing and how they were feeling at that moment. The people having the best time were having sexual relations. Those that were not involved in something in reality were not having a good time. The title of the article is "When the Mind Wanders, Happiness Also Strays."

That study closely parallels what I see in myself, my patients, and "the mass of" people. Given the ubiquity of involvement in negative fantasy, the question arises as to whether Thoreau's "desperation" has its origins in our genetic programming; alertness to negative possibilities would have very high survival value, as we could then take steps to protect ourselves. I suspect we share this tendency with many other animals. If the rabbit in the field was not alert to the possibility that a hungry wolf was in the vicinity, that would be a dead rabbit in short order. In contrast to the rabbit, humans with their remarkable brains can create endless negative possibilities.

We have paid an enormous price for this tendency, for we can react emotionally to negative fantasy with the same intensity as we react to reality. A patient of mine used to describe this as "paying the toll before I get to the bridge." It is this kind of suffering that constitutes the vast majority of suffering. Awareness of when we are involved in negative fantasy can significantly assist us to avoid unnecessary pain. Having an exacting definition of reality can markedly assist that awareness.

It should be noted that the basic evolutionary tendency toward involvement in negative fantasy can be enhanced if the individual is especially genetically predisposed, has considerable underlying guilt, is identified with parents that were particularly prone to negative fantasy, or has suffered an unusual number of real tragedies.

It should also be noted that involvement in negative fantasy is inevitable in a number of situations. For example, if a woman is told there is a lump in her breast, it is inevitable to have the negative fantasy that it might be a cancer. However, the awareness that she is involved in fantasy can assist in moderating the associated inevitable anxiety until she "gets to the bridge."

Further, it should also be noted that involvement in negative fantasy may be one of the ultimate evolutionary sources of humans' enormous creativity. Negative fantasy can obviously stimulate our taking steps to protect ourselves. And the consequently generated complexity could then be utilized for a multitude of creative possibilities.

Interestingly, there may be more synonyms for "fantasy" than any other word: abstraction, anticipation, belief, conjecture, conjure up, construct, conviction, delusion, dream, fancy, feeling, foreboding, forecast, foregone conclusion, foresight, foretell, generalization, guess, hunch, idea, illusion, image, imagination, interpretation, intuition, misinterpretation, myth, notion, opinion, perspective, pipe dream, point of view, premonition, prognostication, projection, prophecy, speculation, superstition, supposition, surmise, theory, thought, version, wonder -- and "I am sure" (another synonym) that this list is not exhaustive.

This vast number of synonyms may simply reflect the fact that we are so often involved in fantasy. Or perhaps they may be an unconscious attempt to avoid recognition of how often our thoughts and words reflect mere involvement in fantasy rather than reality. Of all these words, I generally prefer to use "fantasy" as it has a nice sharp contrast with the word "reality" and may help to maintain consciousness of the critical difference between the two.

Though the recognition of fantasy is so often critical in decreasing unnecessary pain, it often is not enough. Persistent, painful, low-probability fantasies frequently require analysis. For example, the patient I mentioned above who believed when she died she would end up all alone, adrift in a boundless, endless void, had a great deal of guilt about her intensely angry feelings toward her neglectful parents. Her death fantasy can be viewed as a punishing fantasy arising out of her guilt. Recognition that this is very likely the case helps to develop a part of the brain that is observing the fantasy rather than the whole brain "robotized" by the fantasy. And consequently, it helps undermine the fearful affect consequent to the fantasy.

The definition was developed by my patient as a means of aborting his tendency to psychotic manic reactions. But this essay primarily discussed the utilization of the definition in the context of negative emotional reactivity. This essay did not stress the point, but, obviously and very importantly, it may find utility for others who are subject to psychotic reactions.

Over the course of their existence, humans have struggled to find ways to neutralize the negative emotions that accompany the negative fantasies. The invention of the idea of a benevolent God is probably one of the earliest and most enduring attempts. But that idea continues to conflict with questions like one recently put to the visiting Pope by a weeping twelve-year-old Filipino girl: "Why does God allow children to suffer?" Alcohol was also probably one of the earliest attempts to neutralize negative emotions. We currently have a wide variety of other drugs, legitimate and illegitimate, designed to achieve the same objective. Users of heroin particularly report a blissful freedom from negative fantasy. The twentieth century saw the proliferation of psychotherapies, which can be understood, in large measure, as attempts to neutralize negative emotions.

The therapy that most closely relates to this article is "Cognitive Behavioral Therapy" (CBT). It speaks of "negative schema," "cognitive distortions," "irrational thoughts," etc., which obviously are synonyms for what I have preferentially referred to as "fantasies." The incorporation into CBT of a clear definition of reality and some of the related ideas presented in this essay can greatly strengthen its foundation and effectiveness.

Though CBT most closely relates to the material presented in this essay, ideally we incorporate whatever is useful into the therapeutic approach. For example, in the analysis of persistent low-probability negative fantasies, psychoanalytic principles such as the unconscious and concepts of defense can be extremely helpful.

Thoreau had it right; he correctly identified a basic fact: most humans do "live lives of quiet desperation." He did not recognize that this desperation probably has its origins in our evolutionary heritage; alertness to negative possibilities can obviously have high survival value. The individual who can use the definition of reality in the fashion described above can achieve a degree of freedom from some of the negative aspects of that heritage.

2. SOME NOTES ABOUT PSYCHOTHERAPY

I see therapy as a conjoint effort on the part of the patient and myself. Unless there are special contraindications (e.g., the patient is clearly psychotic and will have great difficulty comprehending me), I usually tell the patient exactly what I am thinking, and I urge the patient to do the same with me. We explore together and try to find something useful. In this connection, I offer all kinds of advice invariably with the accompanying caveat: "I take no responsibility whatsoever for what you do with my advice."

Patients frequently kid me about the foregoing: "Oh, here we go again with your disclaimer. You're just trying to protect yourself." My response is usually, "No. It's for your protection. Life is too complicated. I hear about what you are experiencing for forty-five minutes; you are living what you are describing and know a great deal more about it than I do. You have to hang in with your own good head. You can't go blindly with me or anybody else, including doctors, lawyers, or other 'experts.' If you deem the advice appropriate, use it; if it's not, discard it. It's you that have the responsibility for, and bear the consequences of, your actions."

The methods I have developed are in sharp contrast to the way I trained. When I trained, psychoanalysis was in its heyday: it would cure all manner of mental ills, empty out the prisons, bring world peace, etc. Virtually all the major university departments of psychiatry, including UCLA where I trained from 1956 to 1959, were headed by psychoanalysts, and the training was psychoanalytically based. I was taught to stay silent and, when it was appropriate, to offer precise interpretations: "The right interpretation at the right time and the problem would be resolved." I never got it right and neither did my own highly experienced and respected analyst. (How my instructors could teach such nonsense is a real puzzle that will never be resolved -- they are all dead.) As a consequence, I gradually changed my approach to patients, and it has now reached the sharp contrast I am describing. However, make no mistake -- though I've discarded a lot of psychoanalysis, there is much I have retained. Concepts such as the unconscious, repression, and mechanisms of defense are indispensable.

I see therapy as work, and if that is so, then the rules of work should apply; that is, the longer and harder one works, the more one should get done, and if not, why not? So, what does one work on? Ideally we identify what I call "nice clear-cut neurosis" (NCCN). In this connection, ideally the therapist leaves plenty of room for human diversity. So if the reaction is "maybe neurotic," we move on. Examples of NCCN can be found in other articles in this collection: the patient that felt humiliated when verbally attacked, the individuals that hold others responsible for their emotional reactions, persisting in behaviors that are not bringing about the desired result, feelings of inferiority and inadequacy and related tendencies to elevate others, feelings of anxiety and depression that are without basis in reality, etc. Neurosis comes at a cost of unnecessary pain, failure to experience positive emotions, or failure to fulfill potential.

Given the phenomenal complexity of being human, nobody ends up with a perfectly programmed brain; everyone has some neurotic elements of various kinds and degrees. Most neurosis has its origins in early childhood trauma; a second major contributor is identification with parental neurosis. That identification is almost certainly driven by evolutionary forces and is almost certainly shared with other animals. A story I frequently tell in this regard is of a cat in our backyard: When my eldest son was a youngster, he loved cats. He still does. Well, there was this cat that used to wander through our backyard. Whenever anybody got within five hundred feet of that cat, it would go scampering off with its hair standing on end, reacting as if it were about to get slaughtered. That cat was clearly neurotic in that all my son wanted to do was "make nice" and feed it. But my disappointed son would set out saucers of milk that would be gone by the following morning, and we all knew that cat had lapped it up. Well, one day that cat showed up with five of the cutest little kittens you ever wanted to see. And guess what -- whenever a human being came within five hundred feet, the whole crew would go scampering off, hair standing on end, as if they were about to get slaughtered.

That reaction is almost certainly evolutionarily based. Those kittens did not know the potential dangers that exist in the world. They were more likely to survive if they followed their mother's example. The odds are excellent that "follow mother's example" was coded in their genes, and it is likely that we humans have similar parental coding. If you are lucky, you are born with relatively non-neurotic parents, but nobody has the perfect set of parents. We all get stuck with some degree of parental neurosis.

The patient's identification of NCCN is the beginning of its mastery. In order to make this identification, there must be a part of the brain that is, so to speak, standing aside and looking at the neurosis. The more understanding one has of the neurosis, the greater the mastery. However, most neurosis develops early on in life and is deeply ingrained in the neuronal structure of the brain -- it does not get deleted. It is important that one gives up the desire to get rid of the neurosis and resign to its presence. This resignation helps to alert us when it is activated so we can implement the mastery we've developed.

Marked emotional distress nearly invariably accompanies NCCN. That distress is frequently all encompassing. Let me illustrate. I had a patient that was truly brilliant. She occupied a very important position in a complex organization, and a large number of highly educated, sophisticated people reported to her. It was entirely clear that those individuals that reported to her and her superiors held her in very high regard.

Despite her significant accomplishments and all this positive feedback, she was periodically subject to significant periods of feeling like a frightened little girl. A variety of situations would trigger these reactions. One of the most intense reactions took place when the relatives of a very sick friend she was trying to help accused her of ulterior motives. Despite the clear fact that there was not a bit of evidence to support their accusations, my patient suffered inordinately. She had considerable difficulty applying her clearly superior intellect to the situation. She was deeply immersed in feeling like a helpless, frightened little girl, convinced that she was in great trouble.

This reaction was not coming out of thin air. At an early age, she had experienced the death of a deeply beloved father. This enormously traumatic event was compounded by the failure of her family to openly grieve together. Further, her mother, under great stress as a consequence of the death of her husband and struggling to provide financial support to her family, was not emotionally available to my patient when she was young.

When trauma of this sort occurs, it apparently becomes fixed in the neuronal structure of the brain. Though ordinarily not identified as post-traumatic stress disorder (PTSD), it certainly can be viewed as a form of PTSD. Stress of a variety of sorts triggered the neuronal structure with its associated intense and very painful emotional reaction, and once again my patient felt like the frightened, depressed, helpless little girl she had been when her beloved father died.

Though we cannot delete the memory of the very painful event, we can, as in more usual forms of PTSD, decrease the intensity of this patient's painful emotional reactions by having her repeatedly tell the therapist, in great detail, about the experience of the death of the beloved father. The aim of "reliving" this experience is to activate the associated painful emotions. If successful, then there is a significant decrease in the intensity of these emotions, and with that decrease comes greater mastery.

One very interesting aspect of this process is that I have many patients that tell me, "I relive these painful experiences all the time. I cry all the time." I respond with, "To whom?" They inevitably respond, "To myself." I then go on to tell them that doesn't seem to work, that it seems necessary to cry to an understanding, sympathetic other to effect discharge of the tears. Why that should be so is a mystery. It may be that before we humans developed speech, if distressed we would cry to another who comforted, and that process is still necessary to effect discharge of the painful emotion.

Many patients find it helpful to follow the therapist's suggestion to label the complex neuronal structure associated with childhood trauma as the "child self," and to contrast that child self with the "adult self." Ideally that adult self gives up trying to rid itself of the child self and instead becomes the understanding, reassuring parent to that child self -- the ideal parent that was absent when the trauma occurred. But clearly the adult self has to be in charge when it comes to dealing with matters in the adult world.

3. TRAINING ATTENTION

In the essay "Reality and Fantasy," I left out a key therapeutic approach to help deal with an intense flow of negative fantasy; that is, the *training of attention*. Perhaps I left it out because it really does deserve a chapter of its own.

Once one becomes aware of the tendency to get involved in negative fantasy, the next step is to start training attention. I usually will urge my patients to turn attention to reality as defined in the chapter "Reality and Fantasy." I'll point out that, in contrast to their state of "desperation" (recall the Thoreau quote in that chapter), if they are really connected with the reality here in my office, it's quite pleasant. Nobody is threatening us with a gun or a knife, the temperature is reasonable, our chairs are comfortable, there's no earthquake or fire. The company is reasonably pleasant. It's not the greatest moment, but it's not bad at all. I point out that most of life, in this country, is like this moment and that ideally that's where we are living.

Though I've never had it explicated by a member of that organization, I suspect that the Alcoholics Anonymous dictum to "Be Here Now" offers essentially the same advice.

The training of attention is not easy. Attention tends to get captured by negative possibilities and this remarkable brain of ours can generate endless negative possibilities (fantasies). However, we do have a measure of control over the attention mechanism -- a fact, I suspect, most people do not consciously consider. Obviously you can decide to continue to read this essay, turn your attention to the TV, or turn to what's on your mind or what have you. Ideally we enhance that control by practicing at turning attention to reality. Practice, in this instance, won't make perfect, but it can certainly help. In my own therapy, it took me about a year to get a modicum of control over the attention mechanism. I would repeatedly find that I had slipped back into involvement in fantasy, pushed my attention back to reality only to find I slipped back once more. I'm pretty good at it now, but given a situation where a negative possibility has a bit higher probability, the negative fantasies capture my attention, and it takes me a bit of time before I recognize that's the case and go to its rescue. I urge myself, in effect, to "stop paying the toll before I get to the bridge."

I point out to patients that they can practice continually: "Instead of paying attention to what's going on in your head when you leave here, pay attention to the corridor, the elevator, the people on the street, etc."

If I had my way, I would start teaching youngsters control over attention as soon as they could understand what I am talking about. It should be easier to teach them control when they are younger.

As mentioned in the "Reality and Fantasy" chapter, particularly intense, attention-capturing fantasies that make it difficult to maintain a reasonable degree of control of attention may require analysis.

4. IS THAT PHYSICAL COMPLAINT PSYCHOSOMATIC?

In 1962 when John F. Kennedy was President, money flowed readily to programs that taught physicians about psychological factors in their patients. Dr. Jerry Saperstien, a prominent member of the psychiatric staff at the old Cedars of Lebanon Hospital, on Fountain Avenue near Vermont Avenue, obtained a five-year federal grant to instruct non-psychiatric physicians in psychiatry. At the time, I was running the outpatient psychiatric clinic at Cedars, and Jerry asked me to be one of the instructors in that program.

(Incidentally, the staff of Cedars of Lebanon was subsequently integrated with that of Mt. Sinai Hospital forming the now Cedars-Sinai Hospital. The Cedars of Lebanon facility was acquired and is still occupied by the Church of Scientology.)

We developed a very good program. The first year some fifteen physicians attended the evening sessions, the second year about eight, and thereafter zero. Since the grant still had three years to run, I was asked to take it over. I shifted the focus from trying to get the non-psychiatric physicians to come to psychiatry, to taking psychiatry to those physicians. I began to attend and contribute to medical rounds as well as other non-psychiatric meetings in the hospital, and emphasized the availability of psychiatric consultation, etc. And thus was born the Consultation and Liaison Service. An indicator of my success in this endeavor is the fact that I became the only psychiatrist ever elected Member-at-Large, that is, by the entire Cedars-Sinai medical staff, to the Medical Executive Committee.

Surprisingly, I found that more errors were made in diagnosing medical problems as psychiatric than in missing psychiatric problems. The most dramatic example of this was a woman who was in the hospital with a far-advanced cancer of the colon, which ultimately killed her. About eighteen months before this final hospitalization, studies of her gastrointestinal complaints, including colonoscopy, were negative, and it was assumed that her symptoms were psychologically based. Regrettably no subsequent studies were conducted. A repeat colonoscopy might have saved her life. Clearly her symptoms were not psychologically based.

This and other, fortunately not quite so dramatic and tragic, experiences led me to the conclusion that you never assume that physical symptoms are psychological. If after careful medical workup no physical cause is found, then exploration of possible psychological causes is indicated. However, if the physical symptoms change in character or persist for a significant period of time, then the physical studies should be repeated.

The point is that the door is always left open to the possibility that any physical complaint is actually on a physical basis.

5. SOCIAL ANXIETY DISORDER

What is officially diagnosed in the American Psychiatric Association's *Diagnostic and Statistical Manual 5* ("DSM 5") as "Social Anxiety Disorder" (SAD) fits quite neatly into what I have described as involvement in negative fantasy. In this particular case, the negative fantasy is that people will have a negative reaction to the person experiencing the anxiety.

"An estimated 12.1% of U.S. adults will suffer Social Anxiety Disorder at some time in their lives" (https://www.nimh.nih.gov/health/statistics/social-anxiety-disorder.shtml). Though the general designation of involvement in negative fantasy is applicable, given its remarkable frequency, it is, perhaps, deserving of a special designation.

So why should this particular fantasy be so frequent? Some speculations are in order: "Stranger Anxiety" in babies is normal. It begins about six months of age and continues for a year or so. Why should that exist at all? I would guess (have the fantasy) that early on in our evolutionary history, strangers could be very dangerous. Like the chimpanzees reported by Jane Goodall, early humans may have had a propensity for slaughtering one another. The baby's Stranger Anxiety may have evolved as a protective device -- cry! -- if there is a stranger around. SAD may be a continuing manifestation of that early Stranger Anxiety. It would be interesting to survey the parents of patients with SAD to see if those patients have a history of particularly intense and long-lasting Stranger Anxiety.

A few words about my suggested treatment of patients with SAD: The recognition that they are responding to a fantasy is critical. Patients will usually require repeated reminders that they are reacting to a fantasy, as they have not been aware of their propensity to react to fantasy throughout their lives. Acquaint the patient with the above evolutionary theory. The more the patient has some explanation for what they are experiencing, the more they can use their intellect to stand aside from the fantasy they are experiencing.

Training attention to turn away from unhelpful negative fantasy can be a challenging task, but well worth the effort. It, of course, requires that the individual be aware of when they are experiencing a negative fantasy.

Another important issue that is manifest in individuals diagnosed with SAD is their apparent tendency to elevate the other. Otherwise, why would one be so concerned about their opinion? Chickens form hierarchies ("pecking order"), but one chicken is very like another. Just so do human beings form hierarchies, but basically one human is very like another. Ideally there is an end to any elevation or diminishment of any other human being.

Like other aspects of SAD, the tendency to form hierarchies probably has an evolutionary origin. Setting up hierarchies would markedly decrease the amount of fighting in the group and thereby increase its possibility of surviving. The value of these hierarchies in current life is obviously highly questionable.

It should be noted that other factors may enter into SAD, such as harsh long-term treatment early in life.

6. EMOTION, RESPONSIBILITY, AND VERBAL ABUSE

We usually accept, without question, when someone says, "They made me angry." But is that statement usually true?

If someone comes up and punches you in the face for no good reason, I would agree that you are justified in saying, "They made me angry." However, if someone comes up and says, "You are one stupid fool," is the statement, "They made me angry", also justified?

I would submit that that latter statement is not justified. Why? Because depending on the psychological makeup of the recipient of the negative statement, the reaction might be amusement, deep feelings of inadequacy, tearfulness, murderous rage, or what have you.

Recently a patient of mine reported that a woman he knew had intensely verbally attacked him because he, doing his job, indicated that, after careful consideration, the decision was made to not use what this woman had offered his company. My patient's emotional response to her attack was to feel deeply humiliated, angry, and vengeful. He had difficulty accepting that his response was unreasonable.

However, he began to get some insight into his reaction when he went on to state that he had suffered repeated humiliating experiences when he was a youngster because of his small, slight body build. He learned that he could cut down on those attacks if he fought back and made life difficult for the attacker. However, to blindly use this mechanism in the adult business world was certainly not in his best interest -- he would be identified as having a childish reaction, as it certainly was inappropriate of him to feel so deeply humiliated under the circumstances described.

The point is that, in the vast majority of instances, the responsibility for a given emotional reaction rests with the individual experiencing the reaction. To argue to the contrary seems to me to imply that we are like puppets on the end of someone else's string.

Intertwined with this issue of responsibility for emotion is the concept of "verbal abuse," a term that near inevitably gets juxtaposed with, and has significant similarities to, "physical abuse." I would agree that if a child is being verbally attacked by an adult, particularly by an adult the child is dependent upon, then the concept of verbal abuse is applicable. Similarly, the concept of verbal abuse may have validity in the instances where there are infirm or mentally challenged adults. However, the usual case I see in the office is a woman complaining about her male partner's "verbal abuse." I will then usually ask if the partner physically attacks. The usual response is negative. At this point I used to question the patient's use of the term "verbal abuse," as clearly the patient had a variety of options as to how to deal with her attacker and avoid being "abused." But I've stopped doing that as, near invariably, the patient would just be angry with me for not accepting what was generally recognized as "verbal abuse." I've now decided that those patients that use the term usually unconsciously experience themselves as dependent children who cannot effectively deal with the attack. These days I will usually discuss ways that the patient might deal with the attack. The primary method I ordinarily recommend is getting away from the attacker -- to the extent, if necessary, of leaving the house. When we've worked through some of the patient's dependency problems, we might get back to my taking issue with the term "verbal abuse."

Individuals that frequently verbally attack others usually have significant infantile aspects to their characters. They are likely to be very dependent on their partners and to suffer significant feelings of loneliness and abandonment if their partners leave the house. Wishing to avoid these uncomfortable feelings subsequent to their partners leaving the house may compel them to curb their attacks.

7. IN PSYCHOTHERAPY, TALK ABOUT WHAT YOU ARE RELUCTANT TO TALK ABOUT

When I first went into practice (some fifty-six years ago!), I had a patient that I knew was not talking about something that was important. I pushed him to talk about it, and after a few sessions he quit therapy with me. And this at a time when, for economic reasons, I needed patients. In retrospect he made a wise decision; I had no business pushing him.

These days when patients are reluctant to talk about something, I don't push them. I tell them that they have to go at their own rate. I then go on to relate the above story, but also go on to emphasize the importance of talking about what you don't want to talk about: "They are the big green lights in psychotherapy. It looks like areas within that you are reluctant to talk about are more likely to give rise to symptoms."

I then go on to relate the following: The most dramatic example of this I have ever seen was a patient I saw very many years ago. She was a Las Vegas prostitute who was picked up one night by two men and a woman. They took her to an isolated cottage and proceeded to terrorize her: guns in her mouth, guns in her vagina, threatening to dismember her, etc. This horrendous experience went on for about three days.

She came out of that experience totally psychotic. She saw several psychiatrists before she saw me; all of them hospitalized her, but none had been able to help her. I hospitalized her as well. She was so disturbed that I arranged to have her put in a padded room for fear she would harm herself by hurtling herself against a wall.

I told her that she had to talk about what happened. "No! No! No! I can't do that! It was all too terrible! I won't talk about that!"

I told her it was up to her, but if she wanted to stop bouncing in and out of hospitals, she was going to have to talk about what happened.

This interchange went on for several days. She finally relented and rapidly told me what happened. And it was truly horrendous.

The next day I told her she needed to tell me the story again in greater detail. She again expressed intense resistance but again relented.

This exchange went on for many more sessions. But guess what began to happen.

Not infrequently my current patient will guess appropriately: "It began to get boring."

I go on to say, "That's right. How many times can you repeat the same story over and over again and not get bored? This is one of our greatest strengths and one of our greatest weaknesses. On the one hand, it assists us in adapting to all kinds of situations. On the other hand, for example, those Germans that gassed thousands might have been reasonably decent people before their concentration camp experience. But after you've forced hundreds to their deaths, it probably became just another job."

My Las Vegas prostitute stopped being psychotic and left the hospital. She still had significant problems but that ended her bouncing in and out of the hospital. The point is that the attempt to avoid what there was no avoiding resulted in symptoms. This principle seems to apply generally. With my Las Vegas prostitute, it was easy to access the traumatic episode and the associated feelings because it had recently occurred. With most of my patients, the trauma had occurred in childhood, and accessing the associated feelings can be much more difficult. But it is worth the attempt.

Ideally you end up with no area within that you are reluctant to talk about. Being in that position not only decreases the probability of symptoms, but contributes to a solid self-confidence and a sense of internal freedom.

8. IF WHAT YOU ARE DOING ISN'T WORKING, TRY SOMETHING ELSE

The bit of advice given in the title of this essay is patently obvious, but it is astonishing how often it is ignored in personal relationships. Repeatedly I hear patients who in their business affairs strictly adhere to the title of this essay, but fail to do so in personal relationships.

Just recently a patient was complaining to me about his relationship with his wife, which had long been characterized by the two of them vehemently criticizing one another with consequent unhappiness and no change on the part of either one of them.

Whenever I hear this kind of tale of woe, which is with some frequency, I usually tell the patient the following: The most striking example of the failure in personal relationships to "do something else if what you are doing isn't working" that I have ever encountered was a man who consulted me when he was in his mid-sixties. He was having a perfectly miserable time in his marriage of some forty years. Meals consisted of store-bought defrosted platters tossed on the table. His wife would pay no attention to what he had to say, and, in general, treated him with utter disrespect.

Despite the fact that it was to no avail, he had continued over all those years to attempt to placate her, hoping by treating her very well that she would respond in kind.

Now this same man held a high position in a very competitive industry. His organization spent millions searching for solutions to complex problems. He had gained his high position primarily because he was the guy who would review very expensive ongoing research, and not infrequently declare, "Ladies and gentlemen, this obviously is not working; you are going to have to scrap what you are doing and find another direction."

When I pointed out the contrast between the way he operated in his work and the way he operated in his marriage, it was like a very big light went on. I have never, before or since, seen an individual make such a remarkable change. He went home and raised "holy hell" with his wife. Indicative of the marked shift in their relationship was the fact that they had sex for the first time in fifteen years!

9. IRRATIONAL GUILT AND UNWANTED FEELINGS

Louise's mother, who had a long history of psychological problems, had made a suicide attempt when Louise was fifteen years old. The attempt deeply distressed Louise and her family. With some difficulty, Louise told me that she had some very angry feelings toward her mother: "At times I wish my mother had succeeded in her attempt." As a consequence of these feelings, Louise suffered a great deal of guilt: "One shouldn't have feelings like this toward one's mother."

The issue of what I call "irrational" or "neurotic" guilt is extremely common and involves some fundamental and complex issues.

Louise's statement that she "shouldn't have feelings like this" implies that she should have control over her feelings. I responded, "If I could control my feelings, I know exactly how I would feel all the time: on top of the world, loving everything and everybody, feeling totally competent, totally free of all anxiety or any other negative feelings. Maybe once in a while I'd come down for contrast, but I suspect I would quickly go back to my euphoric state." However, the clear reality is that we don't control our feelings. They go on whether we like them or not. Should I have guilt about feelings over which I have no control?

Further, reasonable guilt should have something to do with harm. Louise reacted as if her wish had the power to injure her mother; of course it doesn't. Where is the harm in Louise's wish that her mother had died? The only "harm" is that Louise suffers.

People like Louise do well to use a legal definition when they are experiencing guilt. A reasonable legal system doesn't care what you think or wish; *actions*, that's what counts.

Though Louise may agree that her guilt is irrational, odds are great that she will continue to experience that irrational guilt. But if another part of the brain recognizes her guilt is irrational, it can help to significantly mitigate that guilt. Turning attention (see "Training Attention") away from that irrational guilt may help considerably. Further, deliberately blocking behavior arising from that irrational guilt can particularly diminish the intensity of that guilt. It is as if the brain says, "Well, she's not using this guilt. Perhaps we can let it go into a back file."

Though the recommendations in the preceding paragraph can really help, probably the most effective way for Louise to reduce the intensity of her feelings of guilt is to review in great detail the history of her relationship with her mother, with special focus on her mother's suicide attempt. This helps reactivate the intense underlying feelings and to discharge them, to the extent possible, in the therapeutic situation. Recall the story about the Las Vegas prostitute in the essay "In Psychotherapy, Talk About What You Are Reluctant to Talk About." The principle described in that article obtains in this situation. However, it was much easier in that situation to access the feelings, as they had recently occurred. Accessing feelings from the distant past is invariably more difficult. They require much more time and work, which can get significantly costly. Some patients might benefit from attempting to access the relevant feelings by writing about them in great detail.

10. THE PROBLEM OF DIAGNOSIS IN PSYCHIATRY

Recently, virtually every other new patient I see in my office tells me they have been diagnosed as "bipolar." "Bipolar" is apparently the diagnosis du jour. However, not one of these patients has a good clear history of a full-blown manic reaction, and only a very few have a history for a possible hypomanic (less than full-blown) state.

The issue of diagnosis is very important, as treatment is often contingent on an accurate diagnosis. It would constitute a significant error to treat for bipolarity when that diagnosis is not founded on solid data, particularly because most of the drugs used to treat Bipolar Disorder have potentially serious side effects. Virtually all those patients that come in my office with what they say is "bipolar" suffer from Major Depressive Disorder, which responds well to a combination of relatively non-toxic antidepressant drugs and psychotherapy. When they recover from their depressive episodes, they will, not uncommonly, experience a period of mild euphoria - not surprising in that there is considerable relief in being free of depression. This should not be confused with hypomania.

Where the diagnostic system currently in place is particularly prone to leading therapists in inappropriate directions is the personality diagnoses. When the diagnosis of Borderline Personality Disorder was initially promulgated, I had a patient who fit virtually all the criteria: she was markedly impulsive, her relationships were chaotic, and she had made several suicide attempts. I started treating her after she was hospitalized for one of those attempts. Strikingly, after several weeks of treatment and apparent substantial improvement, I gave her a pass. She immediately, and totally unpredictably, checked herself into a nearby hotel, got into a bathtub, and slit her wrists in another unsuccessful suicide attempt. However, this former patient is now, and has been for many years, a very successful and clearly stable psychotherapist.

The point is, be wary of those personality diagnoses. Each of us is markedly unique and phenomenally complex. This complexity is a reflection of the phenomenally unique and complex brain we all have. Though significant problems may be apparent, you never know, until you've worked with the patient for a considerable period of time, what strengths they may have. As a consequence, the best personality diagnosis is usually "complex human being." A good dictum: "Treat the complex human being, not the diagnostic label."

II. RESIGNATION

My wife and I were recently out to dinner at a favorite restaurant, Chinois on Main, with a couple that we've known for some fifty years. It so happened that a handsome young couple with an equally handsome three-year-old son were seated at the table next to ours. A conversation ensued, particularly sparked by the young mother. They were from rainswept Oregon and were here in sunny (we were in the midst of a drought) Santa Monica on vacation.

The young mother correctly assumed and corroborated that both of us couples had been married for many years and asked how we accounted for our obviously successful marriages. My wife responded with one word, "resignation," and elaborated: "Give up trying to change the partner." She did not elaborate further, but my goal is to do so in this essay, as resignation is a critical issue in relationships. I would dare to venture that a large percentage of divorces have failure of resignation as a core issue.

A great deal of what I write about in this essay derives not only from my clinical work but from my own personal experience. A good deal of the friction early on in my marriage was my struggle to get my wife to be more like me. For example, if I use a cup when I'm through, I put it in the dishwasher. She would just leave it on the counter. For years and with considerable frustration and consequent anger, I tried to get her to put the kitchenware she used in the dishwasher. A similar attempt to get her to close drawers she opened met a similar fate. (What's that song -- "Why Can't a Woman Be More Like a Man?")

I don't know how it happened. I suspect it was consequent to my contrasting objectivity in dealing with couples with similar problems. But I came to the wise conclusion that if I wanted used kitchenware to go in the dishwasher or open drawers closed, there was a simple, easy solution: RESIGN!!! STOP TRYING TO CHANGE HER!!! DO IT YOURSELF IF IT BOTHERS YOU THAT MUCH!!!

In retrospect, that conclusion is apparent, particularly if you are a psychotherapist. People come to you because they want to change something about themselves. Near invariably they find this very difficult to do despite clear-cut recognition of the necessity to do so. Trying to change another -- forget it!!!

Voila!!! That insight really helped. Though I still dislike her doing the sort of things I described, my negative reaction is much less intense. This is so because having given up my attempt to change her, I do not experience the frustration and anger consequent to my failure to get her to change. I made her life and mine much freer of conflict. Resignation has clearly made a significant contribution to our sixty-six years of happy, loving, married life.

12. CHRONIC LATENESS AND SELF-DISCIPLINE

Recently, I saw Charlie for the third time. As usual he was about fifteen minutes late for the forty-five-minute session. I asked him if this tendency toward being late also applied in other situations. He stated that it applied in every aspect of his life, but he was not particularly troubled by the problem; he'd had it his whole life.

Charlie was totally aware of the potential negative consequences of this habit in the business world he was entering, but again did not seem particularly troubled. He went on to tell me that he did not get anxious about making an appointed time the way most people did; he invariably got anxious later than they did. As a consequence of this problem, he had missed airline flights, etc.

I've run into this problem with other patients in the past and have found it very difficult to assist them in changing this behavior. Given how difficult it is to change, I'm particularly interested in how to avoid developing the problem in the first place. And here we enter into a controversial area, as many would not agree with my methods.

The problem of lateness usually begins around age five when we anticipate that the child should be participating in getting ready to go to school. Most children will readily do so. That participation may be gently encouraged by statements like, "Daddy's got his work, Mommy's got her work, school is your work." Children, wishing to identify with their parents, get out of bed, even though it is with some discomfort on cold mornings, and enter into the process of getting ready to go to school. Good behavior is positively reinforced by the parent with statements like, "Oh, what a big boy!" However, some children -- I suspect a small number -- do not respond to positive reinforcement. Why they don't is poorly understood.

Writing about this reminds me of a patient, we'll call her Nancy, I saw many years ago when I used to hospitalize. Nancy's hospitalization had been ordered by a judge after she had been arrested for driving under the influence. He ordered the hospitalization when he saw that this eighteen-year-old woman had a string of arrests for a variety of infractions, none of which had serious consequences.

Nancy had a two-year-younger brother who was a model of good behavior. Nancy's parents were in a state of confusion: "We brought them up the same way, and yet they are so different." And of course, therein lies the problem. Though there is reluctance to compare humans to horses, like some horses require a much firmer hand to learn to accept being saddled, Nancy required a much firmer hand than her parents provided.

Interestingly, Nancy did fine with following the rules in the hospital and was discharged. I stopped seeing her at that point, but subsequently learned that she had done well when she left the hospital as long as she had to periodically report to the judge who initiated her hospitalization. But virtually immediately after Nancy and her parents successfully petitioned the judge to drop the necessity to report to him, her behavior reverted to getting into trouble. Nancy clearly needed a firm hand to assist her in staying out of trouble.

To return to my current patient, Charlie, I strongly suspected that early on in his development, his parents, like Nancy's, did not provide appropriate consequences for failure to exercise self-discipline. Charlie confirmed this suspicion.

If positive reinforcement doesn't work, it is relatively easy for a parent to impose discipline on a youngster. Easy, for one primary reason -- the parent is so much bigger than the child. Once that advantage is lost, the opportunity is lost. The parent who fails to help the child learn self-discipline at the age-appropriate time has failed their responsibility as a parent. They leave the child with the very difficult task of imposing the necessary self-discipline on themselves. The cost of not having that self-discipline can be enormous. I have seen a number of very bright, talented people who were not able to fulfill their potential because they lacked the vital self-discipline.

I would argue that the appropriate treatment of the child who, for example, at age five or so, is not exercising self-discipline by not getting out of bed to get ready to go to school is to make it clear to the child that it is their responsibility to do so. And if the child doesn't execute that responsibility and get out of bed *now*, then the parent will provide "help" to do so. The child will rapidly learn what constitutes "help" and will get out of bed. For "help" in this instance will be forcefully pulling off the child's blankets, firmly grasping the child, and firmly lifting the child out of bed. The experience is clearly unpleasant, and usually this is all the help that will be required. However, if more "help" is required, then the parent provides some.

After this unpleasantness is over, the parent ideally tells the child they don't like to treat the child in this fashion, but that it's vital that the child take on this responsibility -- and that if the child doesn't take on this responsibility, then the parent will have to do whatever possible to help the child learn self-discipline.

13. OBSESSIVE COMPULSIVE DISORDER

I recently saw a bright young man (we'll call him Sam) who suffered from classic severe Obsessive Compulsive Disorder (OCD). He had seen a therapist for several years, but his shame stopped him from telling that therapist (or anyone else) that he suffered from OCD. The fact that he was able to discuss it with me was a very positive prognostic sign. It clearly indicated that he had overcome his shame and thus opened the possibility that someone else might be able to help him.

Ever since early childhood, he had been involved in rituals. He clearly knew the rituals were "ridiculous," but suffered severe anxiety when he attempted to stop them. The anxiety was a response to a fantasy that if he stopped a ritual, some sort of disaster would occur. I suggested that his rituals were an expression of a wish to have the *power* to control whether or not a disaster would occur. He said that he had not considered that possibility before, and he thought that interpretation was correct -- and that obviously, his rituals did not have that power. However, he doubted that bit of insight would help because of the automatic and immediate intense anxiety he suffered when he attempted to stop a ritual.

Sam made it clear that he was not willing to go through any type of prolonged psychotherapy: "I've been through that." It was clear that pointing out that psychotherapies vary would not persuade him, so we turned to medication. Antidepressants of the SSRI (selective serotonin reuptake inhibitor) class are regularly recommended for the treatment of OCD. I have often wondered why they should work in OCD. It struck me while talking to Sam that these drugs, which are regularly recommended for the treatment of anxiety, are effective in OCD because they reduce the anxiety contingent on stopping a ritual. Sam was reluctant to try SSRIs because of his concern about side effects. So what now?

If my theory about the effectiveness of SSRIs in OCD is due

to their anxiolytic properties, then another class of anxiolytic drugs might be helpful. Though these drugs are not ordinarily used in the treatment of OCD, I suggested Sam take alprazolam (Xanax) when he tried to stop a ritual. I explained to him that it was rapid acting and lasted a brief period of time. Sam was willing to give alprazolam a try.

Because of Sam's need to control, I left it to him as to whether or when he would return. He selected an appointment in a month. We would see then if the alprazolam helped him decrease his rituals.

He never did return.

14. RUN A BUSINESS OR DO SOCIAL SERVICE

I have some concern that some might consider me heartless with what I'm about to express, but if that be the case, so be it.

Over the years I've seen a number of cases where the person running an office or a business has been reluctant to rid themselves of an individual who was not performing up to expectations. The consequence is that they spend hours in states of frustration rather than pleasurable productive work.

A related quandary is actually what stimulated me to write this essay. A young man just about to go off to college told me about a computer game he was playing with six other teammates. One of the teammates could not perform at the level of the rest and markedly slowed down the team. However, "he was a nice guy and we did not kick him off the team." It was clearly a very frustrating experience for my patient and I strongly suspect the rest of the team.

I related to my patient that the parallel situation occurred in business and that my near-inevitable response (I cannot think of an exception) is, "You've got to decide whether you are running a business or a social service agency. If you are running a business, then you ought to get rid of individuals that impede the development of that business. You want to surround yourself with people whom you find very effective and who are a pleasure to work with. One way to execute this highly desirable result is to tell all new hires that 'we've got a complex group of people here. Either you fit in or you don't. If you don't, we'll tell you so, and you will have to look elsewhere for work. It will be no reflection on you; you probably will fit in just fine with some other group.'" Attempts by the dismissed employee to inquire about what specifically they did wrong should be firmly dismissed and the "not fit in with this complex group" reason stated again and maintained.

My very bright young computer game player responded with, "What if a friend of yours desperately needed a job?" My response was to reinforce the above approach. However, after further consideration I have shifted to some degree. My bright young man has put me in a quandary. I guess if I had a very successful business and my friend didn't fit in with the rest of the crew, I might try to arrange a "job" that does not impede the rest of the crew. But this situation brings to mind the famous lines Shakespeare in his *Hamlet* has Polonius deliver to his son, Laertes: "Neither a borrower nor a lender be; For loan oft loses both itself and friend."

15. ON PROPER CONDUCT OF EXTRA-MARITAL RELATIONSHIPS

The *New York Times* for May 24, 2015, reported that according to the General Social Survey at the University of Chicago's independent research organization, NORC, the rate of infidelity has been pretty constant for the last two decades at 21 percent for married men and between 10 and 15 percent for married women. Clearly extra-marital sexual relations are common.

Also common in my psychiatric practice is to see the consequences of extra-marital relationships: disrupted marriages and very unhappy people. Remarkably, the most common way that the partner becomes aware of the affair is by accidentally coming across e-mail exchanges between spouse and lover. Obviously, if you are going to have an affair, do not e-mail, text, or otherwise have any written communication with your lover that your spouse can possibly discover.

Second, do not use your credit card when dining or are otherwise engaged with your lover. Credit card and phone billings can be a dead giveaway that you are having an affair.

Third, do not confess. Follow the principle summarized in that old saw about "If they find you in bed with another, tell them they're hallucinating." If that doesn't work, consider asking them, "Whom are you going to believe, me or your lying eyes?" The individual who, prior to discovery of the affair, confesses to the spouse is invariably trying to get rid of their guilt. But such confessions unfairly burden your spouse and come at the cost of a disrupted marriage. If you have to confess, go see your priest; or if that is not your persuasion, see a psychiatrist.

Fourth (which perhaps should be first), be very carefully selective in your choice of whom you have an affair with. It is a very unpleasant experience to have the other person angrily call your spouse and tell them about how the two of you have been having an affair. If it happens, deny it; say that you just don't understand how this person would say such a thing.

Finally, recognize that having an affair carries the significant risk that you will want to leave your spouse and marry your lover. Maximum pain will be experienced if you find yourself in the awful dilemma of being in love with two people, each of whom does not want to share you.

The whole mess obviously becomes immensely compounded if you have children.

Given the significant downsides, maybe you should just forget about having that affair.

16. FEELINGS OF INFERIORITY

Feelings of inferiority are extremely common in patients that consult psychiatrists. They are clearly neurotic. We human beings are like chickens in the barnyard; we tend to automatically establish hierarchies. However, as one chicken is very much like another in all sorts of dimensions -- size, length of life, strength, egg-laying capacity, etc. -- just so is one human being very much like another, albeit without the egg-laying capacity. Chickens, like us, probably exaggerate the differences. Why we form these hierarchies is probably fundamentally evolutionarily determined. Hierarchies tended to keep down the level of fighting within groups, and such groups in our evolutionary history were more likely to survive.

I say they are "clearly neurotic" in that, in addition to inferiority feelings giving rise to depressive states, going blindly along with a hierarchical structure can get us into other kinds of serious trouble. I have over the years seen a number of instances where disaster resulted from blindly following the advice of individuals who tend to occupy elevated positions, like physicians (including psychiatrists), attorneys, teachers, etc. The recipient of the bad advice near invariably will often say something like "It didn't make sense to me, but he was the doctor (attorney, teacher, or what have you), and I assumed he knew what he was talking about."

Ideally we move against that probable evolutionarily determined tendency to elevate or denigrate someone. These tendencies evolved when we lived in relatively small groups. Within nation-states, they have no apparent survival value. Ideally we see others as equivalents. This does not mean that we cannot respect talent, such as a master violinist, but, ideally, we do not generally elevate that individual and assume he has all manner of special ability beyond his violin playing.

In addition to the possible evolutionary forces playing a role, by far the most significant contribution to feelings of inferiority is early abuse by parents. Probably the most severe such case I have ever heard was from a middle-aged male who reported that his father took pride in being able to stop babies (he had several) from crying: he would beat them every time they cried.

The younger the child, the more likely it will fail to recognize the defects of the parents. Young children are too dependent on the parents to see their apparent defects; they need the parent to be a tower of strength and perfection. If the child is not having its needs fulfilled, the problem must be that something is wrong with them. The result can be deeply felt, lifelong feelings of inferiority.

Successful treatment of these feelings is often accompanied by long-suppressed feelings of rage toward parents.

17. GUILT IN ENDING A RELATIONSHIP AND SELF-ESTEEM PROBLEMS

It should be noted at the outset that this essay only applies to relatively uncomplicated relationships of relatively recent origin. The complexity obviously multiplies if the relationship has gone on for some time, there are children involved, the partner is ill, etc.

Arnold and Sylvia had been living together for a year. Arnold, for a number of reasons, had decided he wanted to end the relationship. He had great difficulty following through with his decision. He knew Sylvia did not want to end the relationship and that she would suffer considerable pain if he left her. The potential guilt about her suffering is what was stopping him.

This is not an uncommon situation. But remaining in a relationship you basically don't want can have significant negative consequences. For one thing, you clearly are living in a state of discomfort. For another, that "the truth will out" is near invariably the case. Failure to be truthful to begin with has delayed the partner from finding someone who really does love them. The partner can legitimately claim, "You lied to me and wasted my time." So now you have legitimate guilt.

Is guilt "legitimate" if you decide to leave? Who is responsible for the suffering of the rejected partner? I would maintain that the responsibility rests with the rejected one. (How did you *ever* arrive at that?) The fact is that whenever one enters into a relationship, one runs the risk that the other will reject. If you don't want to run that risk, then don't enter into relationships.

The appropriate response of the rejected one is "Your rejection is painful, but I don't want someone who really doesn't love me. I was suspicious that this was coming, and I should have said something. Well, it has arrived. So I think it's time for you to leave. I'll recover."

That sentence in the above paragraph, "I was suspicious...," merits further comment. If one is accepting of the possibility of rejection, then they will be much more sensitive to the partner's moods and are more likely to be alerted to the withdrawal of the partner. They can take steps to get rid of the partner who really doesn't want to be with them.

That individual who is not accepting of the possibility of rejection is much more likely to have underlying neurotic problems and will suffer inordinately in the face of rejection. Usually these problems will have to do with feelings of worthlessness activated by the rejection and consequent marked drops in self-esteem. Drops in self-esteem are a common gateway to Major Depression; that painful illness and its antecedent drop in esteem clearly require effective treatment.

An adult can never be in the position where their self-esteem is dependent on another. That other may clearly have complex problems of their own that lead to diminishing other individuals. If a drop in self-esteem occurs in an adult, it should be on the basis of some act of the adult that clearly merited appropriate shame and/or guilt. For example, if one smokes cigarettes, then they should suffer shame. That "shame" is equivalent to saying their self-esteem dropped.

Incidentally, of the two partners described, which do you think is much less likely to experience rejection?

18. FOLLOW YOUR BLISS BUT BE PRACTICAL

I've stolen "Follow Your Bliss" from Joseph Campbell. He was justifiably famous for creating that statement. It is excellent advice.

Many of the patients I see are striving to work in some aspect of the film industry. Because of the marked difficulty in achieving success in this industry -- I don't know any industry that is more challenging -- parents frequently discourage their children from entering it. They should heed the advice of Joseph Campbell and do just the opposite; they should encourage their child to follow their bliss despite the fact that the vast majority will not succeed. Failure to follow one's bliss is likely to result in lifelong suffering from the very depressing possibility that "I could have been a contender!" (Probably Marlon Brando's most famous line, which he delivered with mournful, moving intensity in the movie *On the Waterfront*.)

The vast majority of those striving to enter the film industry will gradually become tired of the lack of economic success and decide to move into other fields. But at least they "took the shot," and it is their decision to leave it and not something forced on them by a parent.

A related issue is the failure of some of those struggling for success in highly competitive fields to utilize potentially helpful resources. For them it is a matter of pride; they want to "make it on their own." This is a praiseworthy, but impractical ethic. The problem is that many of their competitors are perfectly willing to use those resources, and thus the playing field is very significantly tilted in their favor. I strongly encourage those entering incredibly difficult fields, like the film industry, to use whatever legitimate help they can get. Your competitors almost certainly will do so.

19. THE MYSTERY OF VERY PROLONGED DISTRESSING REACTIONS WHEN MATES DISCOVER THEIR PARTNER'S EXTRA-MARITAL AFFAIR

Let me make very clear at the outset that in this essay, I am not expressing approval of extra-marital relationships. Instead I am raising a question about the appropriateness of some of the all-too-frequent disasters consequent to their discovery.

A while ago, Andrew discovered that his wife, Carol, had a sexual encounter with Jason. The discovery occurred in the fashion that is so remarkably common -- Andrew found them communicating on the home computer e-mail. Carol became my patient.

It rapidly became clear that the sex was meaningless to Carol. Carol had befriended Jason when they both attended events in which their children were participating. The friendship became very gratifying for Carol in that she could communicate with Jason in a way that she never could with Andrew. That friendship -- of almost two years -- made Carol susceptible to Jason's advances. In contrast to the friendship, the single sexual experience was not fulfilling for Carol.

Andrew was enraged. He expressed wishes to kill Jason, which obviously alarmed Carol, their children, as well as their extended families. He also repeatedly announced his intention to divorce Carol. Andrew and Carol had two children, ages eight and twelve.

Kill someone? Divorce and traumatize their children? Suffer the consequences of the financial hardship so often generated by divorce? How are we to understand this all-too-common reaction when a mate discovers their partner is having an affair? To my mind, it just doesn't make much sense.

Near invariably, the affair is a strong signal of problems in the relationship. In Andrew and Carol's case, it was clear. Ideally instead of potential murder and divorce, it would lead them to get some help for their communication problem. But why is the former so common?

To begin with, let me clearly state that what follows is, in my terms (see the essay "Reality and Fantasy"), my fantasy. With clear evidence that supports another interpretation (fantasy), I am ready to give up on the notions (fantasies) that follow:

Because of its intensity and ubiquity, I am suspicious that the nonsensical reaction is part of our evolutionary heritage. Going far back in evolutionary time, the female who found an exclusive and committed partner was more likely to survive. She had someone to help protect her from predators, help her when she was pregnant and giving birth, and help feed her and their children. The male wanted exclusivity because it was his guarantee that the children he helped raise were, indeed, his.

Those partnerships that had exclusivity as a key foundation were more likely to survive. The accompanying intense emotions helped guarantee that exclusivity and are, in part, manifest in the intensity of negativity that occurs when that exclusivity is breached. Hence Andrew's readiness to kill Jason and divorce Carol when he discovered Carol's infidelity with Jason.

Now clearly things have changed since these emotions evolved. Women no longer require protection from the kind of predators that abounded in those days. Further, women are clearly able to give birth and raise children without an exclusive partner. As far as the male is concerned, if he has a question of whether he is the father, DNA studies are readily available. However, the emotions that evolved in another evolutionary context persist and give rise to some of the most gratifying (love) and frustrating (those consequent to a partner's infidelity) experiences we current-day humans enjoy or endure.

To return to the central point of this discussion, it is my contention that in the case described above, ideally Andrew uses his intellect to override his rage at Carol's infidelity. Instead of being preoccupied with fantasies of killing Jason and divorcing Carol, he should do whatever possible to mitigate the factors that led to Carol's infidelity.

I fully understand how difficult it is to execute my recommendation. The central problem is the marked intensity of the negative emotions generated. There is no button to simply turn them off. They are not easy to deal with. However, I believe it can be done. The first step is the resignation to the existence of these intense negative feelings, and the recognition that, in any event, they will decline with the passage of time. If they don't, there is usually something going on that is not being dealt with (e.g., the blow to one's self-esteem generated by the partner's infidelity). Beyond that, the more one understands the nature of these negative emotions (hopefully assisted by the above), the more one can develop a part of the brain that stands aside from these negative feelings and deliberately avoids the disastrous consequences to self and family should one act on them.

Dealt with appropriately, the incident can be an opportunity for individual growth and an increase in understanding and closeness between the couple.

20. MARRIAGE VERSUS LIVING TOGETHER

When I was a youngster and a young man (1928~1950), virtually no couple lived together outside of marriage. If they did, they certainly would have been said to be "living in sin" and rejected by the community. There has been a remarkable cultural shift in this country: young couples are much more likely to live together before marriage than not. I think this is a good idea. It is easy to maintain a relationship if a couple goes to their separate domiciles at the end of the day. There is nothing like living together to elucidate whether a couple is really compatible; they are in intimate contact through thick and thin. If they find they are not compatible, they can obviously more readily separate than if they were married and have to deal with the finances and legalities of a divorce.

Most couples, after they have been living together for a substantial period of time, get married. But there is a growing group that doesn't marry: "We don't require a piece of paper." However, this arrangement can carry significant risk, especially if there are children.

Heather had been living with Johnathon for fifteen years. She gave birth to two of his children. The relationship essentially ended when Heather discovered that Johnathon had been having a long-standing affair with his secretary. It became clear that Johnathon had made significant commitments to this "other woman" that he was unwilling to forego. The relationship between Heather and Johnathon was over.

Prior to her having children, Heather's career had been moving along quite successfully, but with the birth of her children, Heather became a devoted mother and homemaker, and consequently her career suffered. Meanwhile, Johnathon's career had flourished, and his income had resulted in a very comfortable standard of living that Heather shared.

When legally married people divorce in the state of California, there are very clear laws regarding division of property, alimony, etc.

However, states vary when it comes to common-law relationships. In California, where the couple had always lived, the law is intricate, leaning relatively strongly in the direction of the partners not having responsibility for each other.

The "other woman" pushed Johnathon to effectively not provide for Heather. Heather's economic situation became very precarious. There is no problem adjusting to a standard of living that is moving up; the converse is very difficult. As of this writing, the settlement of the case is still pending. Obviously Heather would have been in a much better economic position had she been legally married to Johnathon. Couples living together without the benefit of legal marriage should consider Heather's predicament.

21. EXAMPLES OF APPROPRIATELY DEALING WITH YOUNGSTERS

By Gittelle K. Sones, Ph.D., Ed.D.

I was driving my three sons, ages three, five, and eight, home from an errand. We had some time, so I decided they might enjoy telling me how to direct the car. To their great and immediate delight, they took turns: "Turn right here!" "Turn left here!" I followed their directions, as long as it was safe, exactly. It was a game we played with some frequency. I assume their great delight had to do with their being in control of something so much bigger than themselves.

My mother never let me do anything that was the least bit dangerous. I had resolved not to do the same with my children. However, when they began to climb trees, it activated significant anxiety in me. I resolved the problem by closing my eyes or turning my back to them. Fortunately, none of them got hurt.

One of our children did not want to go away to day camp when he was seven years old. Instead he said he wanted to build a clubhouse. The people at Anawalt Lumber were very sweet and measured out exactly what he would need. He spent a summer building the clubhouse, of which he was, justifiably, very proud.

One of our children, at about nine years old, struck up an acquaintance with a boy of the same age across the street. One summer day they said they wanted to build a radio. The neighbor boy's parents felt that the boys were too young to undertake such a project. However, I felt it important that they have this opportunity to attempt this complex undertaking and bought them the necessary parts. To the surprise of both sets of parents, the two of them turned out a beautifully working radio.

I should note that all three sons followed in their father's footsteps and became physicians. All three are now happily married. Two of them now have two grown children, and one has three. So we are the proud grandparents of seven wonderful grandchildren and eagerly await our first great-grandchild.

22. APPROPRIATE ROLE OF PARENTS IN DEALING WITH THEIR ADULT CHILDREN

Parental intrusion into the personal affairs of their adult children is a no-no. This includes their choice of career, whom they marry, and how they raise their children. Parents who do intrude have the misguided notion that they know what's best for their children. And they create all kinds of problems with their sons/daughters-in-law.

There may be times when the parent sees an adult child heading toward disaster. In that event, the parent should get the permission of the adult child to speak about the issue. If permission is given, the parent should make clear that they will immediately cease should the adult child want to terminate the discussion. The clear position of the parent should be that they do not want to intrude and that the child is in control.

One of the primary dangers of parental intrusion is that it may activate a regressive rebellion in the adult child. That is, they make a decision that expresses that rebellion rather than effectively dealing with the issue at hand: "You don't think I should marry the town slut? I'll show you! You can't control me!!"

Conversely, parents who are too intrusive in their child's life may create a dependent adult. The adult child continues to look to the parent to be the decision maker. Obviously this is not a good prescription for a successful life. Ideally parents leave any decision to the child as soon as the child is able to make it for themselves:

Child: "What should I do?"

Parent: "What do you think?"

Child: "I'm not sure."

Parent: "Neither am I. What's your best idea?"

The child gives their best idea.

Parent: "Sounds good to me. Why not try it out and see what happens?"

Of course, exceptions may arise. If they do, ideally the parent continues to take a limited role and support the child's independent decision making. If the child protests:

Child: "I know you have an idea about what is best. Why don't you just tell me?"

Parent: "You are right that I do have an idea of what to do. But I'm not at all sure that it is the 'best.' You've got a real good head, and I think you should use it. You may come up with a better idea. You tell me yours, and then I'll tell you mine."

Child: "Okay. But, you know, you can be a little frustrating with your stuff about always trying to be the ideal parent."

23. ON DEATH

I address this issue here because this is a subject that virtually every patient I have seen for any length of time will talk about at some point. Given that's the case, I assume my Dear Reader will be interested in what follows.

Unlike other creatures, as far as we are able to ascertain, humans are the only ones that have clear knowledge that they will die. Personally speaking, I can assure you that knowledge becomes more and more to the forefront as we grow older. We do not like this knowledge and many of us have developed a whole series of fantasies in the attempt to deny our impending demise: heaven, hell, reincarnation, or what have you. A guilt-ridden patient of mine created her own special hellish afterlife: adrift alone forever in an empty, endless void.

When we don't like what is clearly apparent, then *denial* is the watchword. And death is the example, par excellence, of what we don't like, and our consequent denial in the form of usually pleasant, low-probability fantasies is our solution. Now there is not a single shred of evidence to support the notion of an afterlife. It is remarkable to me how individuals of significant intelligence can accept these extremely low-probability fantasies. But there it is and, what the hell, if it gives them some solace, why disturb their reassuring reverie? So, if you, Dear Reader, are one such, perhaps you would do yourself a favor and stop reading now.

For my own part, an adherent to a strict definition of reality, I prefer to live as close to reality as possible. So let's examine the available evidence. If a part of the brain dies, the function that it serves dies. If you have a stroke that damages the motor area on the right side of the brain, you will suffer paralysis of the left side of the body. Suffer damage to Broca's area and you will have great difficulty speaking but will be able to sing just fine. Suffer damage to Wernicke's area, and you will spout gibberish and frequently not be aware you are doing so. Develop Alzheimer's, and you will ultimately lose all sense of self and function. The point is, "No brain, no mind. Dead brain, dead mind."

Some further points: First, if you have Alzheimer's and die, which one of you go off to heaven? The near invariable fantasy is that you go to heaven healthy and remain that way in perpetuity. Second, we are one of God's creatures. Is it not chauvinistic of us to assume we are the only such creature to get into heaven? All those viruses, microbes, flies, ants, cats, dogs, etc. are excluded?

People generally fear death and I certainly, being in good health, don't want to die. Those that are most fearful of death have the fantasy they will experience death. But virtually every night we have an "experience" that is as close to death as we can "experience." If we did not wake from dreamless sleep, we would be dead. The odds are enormous that the "experience" of death can be well compared to dreamless sleep. Dreamless sleep -- is that something to fear?

24. ON CONTROL OF FEELINGS

Generally, people will freely take medication when the doctor recommends it for the heart, lungs, kidney, stomach, or what have you. In contrast, a great many people, perhaps the majority, are reluctant to take medication for significant psychological symptoms such as persistent, very painful, depressive feelings. They have the fantasy that they should be able to control their feelings. It is a blow to their esteem to have to see a psychiatrist and obtain appropriate medication.

If I could control my feelings, I know exactly how I would feel: Wonderful! Loving everybody and everything! Not a care in the world! I can assure you I do not always feel that way.

The clear point is that we do not have the power to control feelings. They go on whether we like them or not. We *do* have the power to control our behavior. And it is obviously critical that we exercise that power.

Like any other organ in the body, the brain can run awry. A very frequent example of this is seen in patients suffering from Major Depression. These individuals suffer terrible negative feelings: life is black, there is no hope. The vast majority of people who suicide are probably suffering from this condition. Fortunately, medical science has developed medications and, certain techniques (Transcranial Magnetic Stimulation, Electroconvulsion Therapy) that can help the vast majority of people suffering from this condition.

So far this discussion is clear and straightforward, but now things begin to get complicated. The central thesis that *we do not have the power to control feelings* remains, but the fact is that people *do* have the power to *not be aware* of their feelings. And to add to the complexity, they usually are not aware when they exercise that power.

To expand on that preceding paragraph, there certainly are times when we may, for example, feel angry but deliberately choose to ignore that anger, as expressing it can interfere with our accomplishing some higher-priority task. We'll express the anger later when there is no cost. Such conscious, deliberate ignoring of feeling comes at no significant *psychological* cost.

What does come at a psychological cost, and frequent other costs, is when we are *not* aware of feeling. One of the more extreme examples of this I have seen was a woman who had a casual relationship with a man who showed up one day at her apartment with his belongings and asked to move in. He was financially desperate, she felt sorry for him, and permitted him to do so. He found work, she wanted him to leave, he was reluctant to do so, and persisted in remaining despite her now telling him that she wanted him out. Because she was not aware of the intense anger generated in this very frustrating situation, she did not force the issue by, for instance, threatening to call the police to get him out. She clearly let herself be taken advantage of in this situation, and this had been a lifelong pattern.

Such patterns do not come out of thin air. They are usually a consequence of early childhood trauma. In the instance described above, she had a very angry father that would not tolerate any expression of anger on the part of his children. All anger was immediately, and harshly, squelched. The consequence was marked repression of any angry feelings. This set in place that lifelong pattern.

Changing this lifelong pattern is not easy. However, it can be done. With the assistance of the therapist, the patient was encouraged to remember the frightening incidents with the father in detail. If successful in doing this, the childhood fear was recalled but was now accompanied by an adult rage at the father for his inappropriate treatment of his children. Access to anger was now available to her. She could now use her anger to take appropriate care of herself and no longer be taken advantage of.

Repressed feelings seem to occupy space in the brain. Access to, and ventilation of, those feelings seems to free that space for more creative activity. The consequence can be a feeling of internal freedom and increased self-confidence.

25. SOME SOUND ADVICE IN DEALING WITH VERY ILL OR DYING PATIENTS

My experiences as a Consultant and Liaison (C&L) Psychiatrist (see Chapter 4, "Is That Physical Complaint Psychosomatic?") working in a general hospital obviously brought me in contact with very ill and dying patients. Once again, the primary lesson was "Do not generalize; stop looking for simplistic formulas in dealing with complex human beings." Formulas like "Always tell the patient the truth, whether they want to hear it or not" can be very destructive. Patients who were making a relatively effective adaptation to illness when told the "truth" can suffer marked anxiety. And that anxiety can be problematic, not only for the patient, but also for the treating medical staff. Further, given the marked complexity of human beings, any given patient may not conform to what the "truth-teller" sees as "truth."

The patient has to be carefully evaluated, and that careful evaluation should govern what information the patient is told. Certainly, the patient that clearly states they want to hear all available should be told just that. But the physician should stay alert to communications that indicate the patient has had enough. However, the wish of the patient who does not want to be told negative possibilities should be respected.

One of the most interesting consults I did while running the C&L Service dealt with a man who had been told he had a lethal cancer that almost certainly would result in his demise within a period of months. The problem was that the man was overjoyed. During my interview with him he told me that he was a member of a Jehovah's Witnesses group that believed if you lived the right kind of life, you would, on your death, be at the right hand of God. He was convinced that he had led the right kind of life. Hence his state of near manic pleasurable excitement: he was on his way to be at the right hand of God.

I told his doctors that he did not require psychiatric treatment.

26. PSYCHOTHERAPEUTIC TREATMENT OF PSYCHOTIC REACTIONS

When I was in training to be a psychiatrist, I was taught that the appropriate treatment of psychotic reactions was to help the patient "repress" the reaction. Now this makes no sense whatsoever. How can you possibly forget such a climactic, unusual reaction?

I, relatively early on in practice, went in the totally opposite direction. And though these days the vast majority of these reactions are treated with anti-psychotics, I yet think it critical that, in addition to the drugs, a thoroughgoing exploration of the reaction be undertaken.

Many therapists are fearful of undertaking such investigations. They apparently are afraid they will "reactivate" the psychotic reaction. Ideally therapists that are not comfortable with such investigation should refer the patient to a therapist that is comfortable. One of the real concerns is that, subsequent to having such a reaction, patients will tend to see themselves as "crazy" and tend to isolate themselves and experience life-threatening depressive states. This is more likely to occur if individuals, and especially their therapists, want to avoid discussion of the reaction. It is extremely important that the patient recognize that a psychotic reaction is one of the ways that human beings can react; it is part of our humanity.

The investigation of the psychotic state is very similar to the analysis of a dream and can often provide deep insight into underlying issues.

One important caveat: Those patients that are very resistant to exploration of their psychotic reactions should not be pushed. Though there are rare exceptions, in general patients should not be pushed. In this connection, I usually tell the patient the following: "You are more likely to make progress by talking about those things you are reluctant to talk about because those things are more likely to give rise to psychological problems. But you have to go at your own rate." When I first went into practice, I had a patient who I knew was not talking about something that was very important. I pushed him and he wisely left therapy, and this at a time when I really needed patients. So now I don't push. I tell patients, "Areas you don't want to talk about are big green lights in here. You're more likely to make advances in therapy when you talk about what you don't want to talk about. But you have to go at your own rate." (Also see "In Psychotherapy, Talk About What You Are Reluctant to Talk About.")

27. ANGER

For many years now I have defined anger as "the normal, healthy reaction to the frustration of a wish." Minor wish frustrated, minor anger; major wish, major anger. We share this reaction with many other animals; pull food away from a hungry dog, and you are liable to get bitten. If a patient describes a frustrating situation but is unaware of their anger, the assumption that the patient has a problem experiencing anger has high probability.

A Freudian notion that depression is a consequence of repressed anger has been around for a long time. At one point in the 1950s they even experimented with having hospitalized, depressed patients scrub floors with toothbrushes; the notion was to thereby activate their anger and alleviate their depression. I never did hear of that approach having salutary effects.

Current opinion tends to emphasize the physiologic aspects and drug therapy of severe depressive states. However, I still see a significant role of psychological factors, especially those consequent to drops in self-esteem, usually secondary to financial losses or losses in the romantic realm. However, on occasion it does seem that the old notion of depression as consequent to repressed anger does seem to be the case. And the task then facing the therapist is to assist the patient to become aware of their anger.

This usually is not easy, as patients with this problem have usually had it near lifelong. It may come about via identification with a parent who massively repressed anger. However, in my clinical experience, it more likely is a result of an abusive parent. As a consequence, very early in childhood my patient, fearful that severe punishment would follow any expression of anger, unconsciously massively repressed that emotion.

I will usually spell out the complexity of the problem to the patient and encourage them to deliberately look for anger when in a frustrating situation. In addition, in the therapy sessions I urge the patent to carefully review the history of life with the abusive parent. Following that suggestion, the patient will often go through a recitation of events. Such recitations won't help. I'll point this out and then encourage the patient to attempt to *relive* the painful situations. In so doing they may break through the long-standing repression and connect with the underlying anger.

I would again emphasize the difficulty of this task. It usually requires seeing the patient more than once a week for a long time.

It's now been many months since I wrote the above. I return to this essay because today, July 14, 2017, I saw a patient who told me of a relatively unusual problem dealing with anger. She was very concerned about whether something was wrong with her because she frequently found herself very angry at her thirteen-year-old daughter. She felt that she should be more "empathic." Responding to my question as to what her daughter did that elicited the anger, the patient described severely hysterical behavior on the part of the daughter, behavior that was clearly extremely frustrating.

When I told my patient of my definition of anger (see above) as "the normal, healthy reaction to the frustration of a wish," she immediately experienced significant relief: "I thought there was something really wrong with me."

It should be noted that the patient had another child who was without any such symptoms. Further, the patient had sought psychiatric help for her disturbed child without success. She eagerly followed my advice to have her daughter seen at UCLA where the resources for evaluation and treatment of the very complex problems of her daughter would more likely be available.

28. ON LYING

I had serious questions about including this chapter in this book. I was concerned that it would lead some readers to conclude that I was advocating becoming a liar. Let me make it perfectly clear: I am not advocating becoming a liar. Individuals who gain reputations for lying will not be trusted and will suffer a deserved and painful ostracism by their fellow human beings.

The story of George Washington and his confession to chopping down the valued cherry tree is an appropriate story for *children*. It is enormously important that we teach children not to lie. If, for example, six-year-old Johnny was asked whether he and his friend were lighting matches in a household storage room filled with flammable material, and he lied, he might at some point put himself and the family in grave danger. It is vitally necessary to establish a clear ethic in children that lying is forbidden.

However, there are times when it is appropriate for *adults* to lie, and the failure to do so can cause grave consequences for them and their loved ones. I, rather facetiously, made reference to lying in the essay in Chapter 15, "On Proper Conduct of Extra-Marital Relationships." But the fact is that over the years I have seen a number of instances where the adulterer could have saved themselves and their family a lot of grief had they simply lied.

The specific situation that stimulated my writing this essay was a session with a patient whose mother, who lived in Argentina, was visiting the French Riviera with her boyfriend. The mother wanted my patient to visit her there. Now my patient, for good and sufficient reasons, never got along with her mother. Further, she really disliked her mother's boyfriend. In addition, my patient could ill afford to pay for the trip. This, of course, all added up to my patient not wanting to make the trip.

However, my patient knew that if she told her mother that she didn't want to make the trip, an overt and very ugly battle would ensue, an outcome my patient wanted to avoid. So, she was planning to make the trip. My patient had not considered lying to get out of this unpleasant predicament. She was still bound in the childhood ethic: "Never tell a lie!"

When I pointed out the obvious convenience of lying in this situation, she was initially taken aback. However, she was able to apply her good intelligence to the issue and move herself toward not being so tightly bound by the childhood ethic of "Never tell a lie!"

The problem then shifted to the necessity of having the lie being as foolproof as possible. It is very embarrassing to be caught lying. Further, clearly lying should be kept to a minimum. The more frequently one lies, the higher the probability that one of those lies will turn out not to have been "foolproof."

The patient came up with the plausible possibility that there was a good job potentially hers, but she had to be available for interviews, etc., and therefore could not make the trip.

I feel compelled at this point to reiterate my "disclaimer": I take no responsibility for whatever happens to you if you lie and are found out. You are on your own. (See also the Disclaimer and the first two paragraphs in Chapter 2, "Some Notes About Psychotherapy.")

29. THE SELF-ESTEEM SYSTEM

In this essay, I will share with you, Dear Reader, how I got to my current confused state on this very, very complex subject.

The notion of a "self-esteem system" grew out of my experiences with patients whose symptoms involve self-esteem. Probably the most crippling effect on self-esteem is seen in patients suffering from Major Depression. They feel totally worthless. This feeling of worthlessness is one of the key factors contributing to suicide attempts, which are more common in this condition than any other, including far-advanced cancer.

Less crippling, but certainly limiting, are the consequences of a fragile self-esteem. This can find expression in many different ways. One common way is the reluctance to expose the self to rejection. I commonly see patients who are hungry for a relationship but will not approach someone they find attractive for fear of rejection. This is an example of what I have called, in other essays in this book, "nice clear-cut neurosis." Clearly the risk of rejection ought not to stop someone from approaching someone they find attractive. If that one rejects, so be it and on to the next. The individual who is freely able to be rejected is certainly much more likely to find a suitable partner than the individual who does not approach out of fear of rejection. Which reminds me of one of my favorite quotes from the poet Theodore Roethke: "Those who are willing to be vulnerable move among mysteries."

Another common expression of this same neurotic problem is that those individuals will not risk showing their writing, painting, interest in running for public office, or what have you. They fear rejection and a blow to their self-esteem. They consequently miss the opportunity to have a more fulfilled life.

Individuals that have deep feelings of inferiority consequent to some aspect of their physical appearance are frequently seen in psychiatrists' offices. Their attempts to surgically correct what they perceive as some sort of deformity are very often to no avail; they continue to perceive themselves as unattractive and continue to suffer deep feelings of inferiority.

Related to that last paragraph is the very frequent neurotic failure of individuals with some *real* infirmity to reveal that infirmity by getting a hearing aid, using a walker or wheelchair, etc.

Another common expression of low self-esteem is the tendency to blindly go along with "expert" advice from psychiatrists and other doctors, attorneys, college advisors, or what have you, even though the advice made no sense. Following such advice can have severe negative consequences. Don't do it! Seek other consultation if your expert's advice doesn't make sense or would place limits on your ambition.

One particularly tragic aspect of the self-esteem system is that it can get programmed negatively as a child, and feelings of inferiority will then persist throughout life. Clinically, it frequently seems that this programming takes place not only through direct attacks on the child, but as a consequence of the child's inability to see parental defects. The young child's total dependency on the parent requires the child to see the parent as a tower of strength. If the child is not getting what it wants and needs from the parent, the defect must be in the self, not the parent. The so-called "adolescent rebellion" occurs when the child begins to have enough independence to recognize parental defects, but sadly the damage to the child's esteem has already been done.

Problems relating to low self-esteem certainly are much more common than those relating to elevated self-esteem. Unrealistically elevated self-esteem is seen in Narcissistic Personality Disorder. These individuals rarely seek treatment, will value their own assessments of complex problems over individuals who have studied those problems for many years, etc. It is said of these individuals that they have deep underlying feelings of inferiority, as they take such offense if they are contradicted. That may be so, but some of these individuals may just be angry because someone dared to question them.

Problems related to elevated self-esteem are seen most dramatically in patients suffering from manic reactions. Not infrequently such individuals become psychotic and see themselves as having a special connection to God.

Interestingly, manic reactions, in contrast to Major Depressions, are very rarely seen in isolation. They usually take place in Bipolar Disorder where the individual cycles, with varying rates of occurrence, between the "poles" of mania and depression.

The very term "Bipolar Disorder" raises the question of what is going on between poles. It is this illness, in particular, that led me to the theory that mania and depression are at opposite ends of a biologically based "self-esteem system": the clinical examples given above are examples of difficulties arising primarily from that system, with Bipolar Disorder the most dramatic of those difficulties.

So why would we have evolved with such a biological system? Though the system is much more complex in human beings, I suspect that we share elements of it with a number of other animals. For example, groups of chickens will form "pecking orders," social hierarchies that cut down on the fighting for resources. Most primates, including humans, form social hierarchies as well. I suspect we developed them when we lived in small groups for the same reason as chickens: to cut down on fighting. The complexity in human social hierarchies results from the fact that different human cultural groups "program" the basic system with different criteria. What I have written in this paragraph is almost certainly a gross oversimplification, but it will do for my purpose.

The point I want to drive home is that ideally, we use our powerful intellects to recognize and, in a sense, to separate ourselves from this biological system, as it has little value in current-day human societies. That we recognize when that system is operating and, for example, giving rise to feelings of inferiority. That we recognize that just as one chicken is very like another in terms of their fundamental abilities and characteristics, just so is it with ourselves and other human beings. That though we can admire, for example, the skill of a great musician, we do not generally elevate (or denigrate) them or anybody else. That we not permit feelings of inferiority and associated feelings of anxiety to interfere with developing our full potential, including approaching those to whom we are attracted.

I fully recognize the profound difficulty of executing what I am recommending. The problem is the intensity of those negative feelings. One might be able to decrease some of that intensity by careful exploration of the origin and consequences of those feelings. However, odds are that they will persist to some degree. Resignation to their presence helps, as it prepares the individual to deal with them. The most effective method of dealing with them is the deliberate acting from a realistic appraisal of any given situation. It is as if the brain says, "Well, they are not using these feelings of inferiority anymore. So I guess we can put them into a back file."

Never underestimate the power of the intellect in dealing with this or any other situation.

30. THE TENDENCY TO GENERALIZE ABOUT COMPLEX HUMAN BEINGS

"All men want you to give them a hard time. Play hard to get, then he'll be interested."

"I know she will reject me. There is no point in approaching her."

The above two paragraphs are common cases of fantasy. However, individuals that believe such statements very rarely recognize they are involved in fantasy. The consequence, of course, is marked limits on their potential for fulfilling relationships.

Ideally we give up looking for simplistic formulas in our dealings with our fellow infinitely complex human beings. We resign ourselves to the obvious fact that some of them will have positive reactions to us and others negative, just as we have positive and negative reactions to others. We freely and respectfully approach others openly and are willing to run the risk of experiencing a negative reaction.

If the pain of a potential negative reaction is so great that it stops one from approaching others, that is a clear indication of a need for psychotherapy.

31. KEY TO A HAPPY MARRIAGE

Jimmy Durante made the song "Make Someone Happy" famous. However, he did not go into any detail as to how that excellent advice can be executed. In this series of essays, I will attempt to give some suggestions as to how to go about making someone happy. Probably the most important suggestion was already expressed in the essay in Chapter 11, "Resignation." The suggestion I offer now is also difficult to execute, but the payoff in terms of a happy partner can be significant.

Every time you are critical of something your partner is doing, don't voice it. This is obviously particularly important if your partner is very sensitive to criticism. Voicing the criticism usually leads to an unhappy partner, and, depending on a host of issues, can lead to lengthy arguments without an effective solution.

If you deem it critical to communicate the criticism, it can often be more effective to write your partner about what is disturbing you. Written complaints frequently are more carefully attended to than verbal, particularly if they are accompanied by clear statements of how much you love your partner.

If written statements are ineffective, you might consider conjoint therapy. If you or your partner responds to that suggestion with "I don't believe in psychotherapy," my response is "I don't *believe* in psychotherapy either. It is not a question of *belief.* Either psychotherapy is useful or it is not. The only way to find that out is to try it. If it helps, then you are a damn fool if you don't use it. On the other hand, if it doesn't help, you are a damn fool to continue."

What complicates the above is the fact that psychotherapy is not an exact science. Psychotherapies vary dependent on the individual therapists. The task of the patient is to find a therapist with whom they can effectively communicate.

If your partner resolutely refuses to explore the possibility that psychotherapy might be useful, you have a major problem on your hands – a problem to which I have no solution.

32. DEPRIVED OF THE MOTIVATION OF MONEY

I practice in a community where there are a significant number of wealthy people. Periodically, I will see a child of one of these families who has not come anywhere near fulfilling their potential. Frequently they are significantly involved in using drugs -- usually marijuana. Oftentimes they have graduated from college. But since college, they are not involved in any particularly productive or creative endeavor. They are essentially adrift -- their economic needs liberally provided for by their wealthy parents. They consult psychotherapists because they are unhappy. They are usually very difficult to treat.

Unlike those individuals that lack self-discipline, they do have an ability to proceed effectively when clearly required -- witness the fact that they often have completed college with good grades. What then is the problem?

I would submit the possibility that the problem usually is a lack of motivation. Some fortunate individuals know what they want to do from an early age: become a doctor, do research in how weather works, accumulate a fortune, become a police detective, or what have you. Problems arise in those individuals who, sadly, never had a specific goal they were interested in pursuing, and, in contrast with less wealthy individuals, they are deprived of the motivation of money.

I say "deprived" because if you don't have wealthy parents, you are near invariably significantly motivated by a desire to make money. You want to have a decent place to live, afford decent food, have convenient transportation, etc. The desire to make money gives your daily life purpose and meaning. And, ideally, it leads you to use your creativity to get involved in enterprises that not only make you money, but are fulfilling in their own right. By indiscriminately providing money to their children, wealthy parents run the risk of depriving their children of this critical motivation.

With this in mind, wealthy parents ideally are discriminating in the way they provide money to their children. Certainly, providing money for education and medical care is clearly indicated. But ideally, parents get the message across to their children that it is anticipated that they will become self-supporting and will be moving out of the parental home and establishing homes of their own.

Indiscriminate provision of money can have profound consequences that follow from this lack of motivation. The aforementioned move toward drugs can develop into serious problems. The failure to develop some career can lead to feeling inferior to contemporaries that are developing careers, and those feelings in turn can lead to Major Depressions. Further, these individuals will not be seen as desirable life partners.

There are numerous exceptions to what I am suggesting in this essay. There certainly are children that are appropriately supported for long periods of time. Obviously children physically or mentally compromised may require lifelong support. Children seriously pursuing certain creative endeavors may merit long-term support, etc.

In summary, it is apparent that given the downside consequences, parents have to be alert to the possibility of depriving children of the motivation of money.

33. DEVELOP A BUSINESS OF YOUR OWN

During my years of listening to patients, complaints about work problems have come up with marked frequency. Usually those complaints center around the people to whom patients report. Other complaints center around the dullness of the work, the lack of opportunity for advancement, the low pay, etc. Frequently the complaints have compelled some of those patients to search out new jobs. Generally, they have found this task to be an onerous one.

However, the people that near invariably are enjoying their work are those who have developed businesses of their own. Their time is their own, they are the boss, and they generally are making a lot more money. So naturally I encourage patients to develop a business of their own if at all possible. They may not be able to do so immediately, but they obviously should stay alert to future possibilities.

34. PROPER CONDUCT OF MARITAL (OR NON-MARITAL) SQUABBLING

A very common situation I see in my office is a married couple squabbling over something or other. Invariably, neither is listening to the other; they each are trying to get their point of view heard by the other without success.

I usually forcefully intrude, point out the obvious, and firmly suggest that they take turns and quietly listen while the other speaks. Despite my suggestion, it is commonplace for the "listener" to defensively intrude at critical points. I will then intrude again and insist on them waiting their turn. I also suggest that if there is some point they felt very important to address when it is their turn, that they write it down, and I offer pen and paper. I point out that this is obviously the model they should use at home.

Arguments over what actually occurred are a waste of time. The couple must resign to the differences in perception of what happened. Neither has a recording of what happened.

In addition to the above, I usually suggest the following for home squabbling:

Leave off the exchange if it is getting heated. Try returning to it when you both have cooled down.

If you are finding it impossible to communicate verbally, try writing to one another.

If your partner is unable to accept that differences of perception or point of view exist, you have a serious problem on your hands. Consult with a good psychiatrist; they may be able to help.

If your partner refuses to see a psychiatrist, this is a really bad prognostic sign. Individuals that refuse to speak to a psychiatrist are usually very depreciating of the psychiatrist. But what is the real reason they won't go? After all, what is there to lose? The psychiatrist may help or not. Perhaps they are deeply fearful of what they or the psychiatrist might find out.

If you are clear you are wrong, acknowledge that's the case and go on from there. However, hold your ground if you believe you are right. Your perception or point of view is as valid as your partner's.

Getting physical is a deal-breaker. Get away as rapidly from the physically abusive partner as possible.

Finally, and very importantly, do not discuss the problem with relatives or acquaintances. They usually will take your side and can enormously complicate an already-complex situation. Further, they may continue to be alienated from the partner long after you and the partner have reconciled.

August 17, 2017, addendum: A patient of mine reported today that she used the writing technique referred to above to good effect and added an additional two good effects: First, she found that writing the problem and her point of view down virtually stopped her tendency to obsess about the problem. Second, if the problem arose again, she planned to simply hand her husband a copy of what she had previously written.

35. IDENTIFICATION WITH A DISTURBED PARENT

David came into his session raging. He had just got off the phone with his mother. "She is totally irrational. I can't tolerate talking to her." David then went on to describe some of his mother's behaviors. And she does have some unique, compulsive, bizarre rituals, some of which I'd never heard before in some sixty years of practice. Sadly, I cannot share these with you because of patient confidentiality.

My Dear Reader might guess what my patient suffers from. If you guessed he suffers from irrational, compulsive behavior, you guessed right. However, none of his symptoms are bizarre like those of his mother, and, in contrast to his mother, he is acutely aware of their irrationality.

So what's going on here? Something he completely rejects in his mother, he has going on within himself. Are there genes causing irrational behaviors? Though that's a possibility, I doubt it. Genes are usually in the organism because they have survival value, and the survival value of compulsive irrational behavior is highly questionable.

But genes in another way may be involved here. Allow me to divert to what, on first glance, seems unrelated: My eldest son, when a youngster, loved cats -- still does. There was a cat that wandered through our backyard. My son would try to approach it with a saucer of milk, but if that cat just glimpsed the presence of a human being, it would go scampering off, its hair standing on end, as if it were about to be slaughtered. My son would leave the saucer of milk outside. It would be gone in the morning and we knew that cat had lapped it up.

Well, one day that cat showed up with five of the cutest kittens you ever wanted to see. Well, guess what. Whenever a human being appeared, the whole group would follow their mother, scampering off, hair standing on end, as if they were about to be slaughtered.

The kittens do not know the ways of the world. They are probably genetically programmed to follow their mother's lead. If she is frightened, they react with fear. We humans probably share the same genes.

To get back to my patient, if his mother repeatedly used irrational rituals, my patient would not as a youngster see them as irrational. Instead he followed in his mother's footsteps and developed irrational rituals of his own. I shouldn't be surprised that she verbally reinforced this behavior. It is only as David became less dependent on her that he became very annoyed with her irrationality.

But the damage was done. David, despite his recognition of their irrationality, could not stop his own rituals. They markedly interfered with his developing any kind of career despite his clearly superior intellect. It was this state of affairs that led him to seek out treatment.

Treating someone whose neurosis has such deep roots is a challenge. We will be seeing if a combination of drugs and psychotherapy can help. Hopefully he will be able to turn some of the rage he experiences with his mother to separate himself from his "mother within."

36. HOW TO MAKE A WOMAN HAPPY

"Once you have found her never let her go" (from the musical *South Pacific*), and it is mandatory that she feels the same way about you. From that point forward frequently tell her that you love her and that you would move heaven and earth for her. The rest takes care of itself. However, a few additional bits of advice are in order:

Never, never forget an anniversary, her birthday, or Valentine's Day.

Insist on paying for her whenever you take her out.

Open and close doors for her. Have her go through the door before you do.

Tell her frequently that she is far and away the most beautiful woman in the whole wide world.

Wait on her. Most women really enjoy that and she will return the favor.

If she welcomes being kissed and held, do so frequently.

Even if you've got a lousy voice, sing love songs to her. Surprise her and sing them on her voice mail on anniversaries, etc., and intermittently on no special occasion.

Tell her she's the sexiest woman alive. Get clear about what she desires sexually and provide the same. She will return the favor.

Continue to play with her, especially and including sexual play, no matter how old you are. And my wife notes, "That's how to make a man happy too."

Some play takes on very childlike characteristics. It is usually only in the context of long-standing intimate relationships that such play can take place. Ideally partners are freely able to indulge one another in such play. Partners unable to be involved in such play often suffer from activation of painful childhood memories if such play is initiated. Ideally they seek therapy for the problem.

All this is summarized and more beautifully expressed by Jimmy Durante in his classic song "Make Someone Happy." It's on YouTube.

37. UNWANTED NEGLECTED CHILDREN

A very frequent problem I see in the office can often be traced back to this issue of not really being wanted. Young children cannot possibly see the parent as having a problem. They are too totally dependent on the parent. To see parents as defective would activate overwhelming anxiety. If they are not getting the loving responses they require, they near inevitably see the problem as something defective about themselves. Lifelong, deeply felt feelings of inferiority and inadequacy often can be traced to not being wanted to begin with. And these feelings are usually accompanied by feelings of anxiety and depression.

Treatment of these patients is often very difficult and time-consuming. Rarely do they have the time and funds to support the intensive treatment they require. An approach I will take, with varying success, is to try to separate the competent, effective, adult reality-testing part of the self from the unhappy neglected child part of the self, and to have that adult part take an understanding, compassionate attitude toward that neglected child part of themselves -- to be that loving parent to themselves that they never experienced.

Simultaneously it is critical that they become acutely aware of that child part of themselves and not permit it to "run the show." That child part may manifest itself, for example, in being deeply immersed in feelings of inferiority and inadequacy, in being unreasonably angry or guilt-ridden, or in elevating others and blindly following bad advice and the adults not using their own good heads.

Therapy is invariably marked by repeated failures to stay in that adult position. This is to be anticipated, given that these individuals have been operating from that neglected child position so much of their lives.

Critical tools in dealing with these, and with most patients, are outlined in the essays in Chapter 1, "Reality and Fantasy," and Chapter 2, "Some Notes About Psychotherapy."

If the patient resigns to the complexity and difficulties involved, they can often make effective progress. But again, it ain't easy.

38. ADRIFT WITH NO CLEAR VOCATIONAL PATH

Individuals who know what they want to do at an early age are fortunate. An ambition to be a doctor, dancer, astronaut, or what have you can provide near lifelong direction and motivation. However, most individuals are probably not that blessed. I suspect that many members of this less fortunate group do find their way to some reasonably fulfilling occupation. However, what I frequently see in my psychiatric practice are individuals that have not found their way; they are adrift and have accompanying depressive emotions.

Whenever I think of these individuals, I am reminded of a *New Yorker* cartoon published many years ago. This particular cartoonist frequently portrayed a little bearded man in a variety of situations. In this particular cartoon, the little man holds some paintbrushes. His beard trails for a long distance across the floor while he is staring at a huge blank canvas.

Ideally our little man *paints* instead of staring at an empty canvas. If he doesn't like what he has produced, then ideally, he whites out what he painted and paints anew. Just so, my psychiatric patient, instead of staying adrift, ideally *takes a direction*. If the path chosen is not fulfilling, then ideally they choose another path. In doing so, my patient hopefully finds something that fulfills them. And even if they don't, at least they have the hope of finding a fulfilling path, instead of staying depressingly adrift.

39. TURN ADVERSITY INTO ADVANTAGE

The title of this is the Sones family motto. I'm not sure whether or not that qualifies me to be a plagiarist, particularly in view of the fact that I invented that motto. In any event, as adversity affects all our lives at one time or another, it is an excellent motto. And I am sure the Sones family will not object to my making it available to you.

A few years ago, I saw a patient who might significantly benefit from my having that motto readily available. She was Chinese and was studying computer-related aspects of business at the University of Southern California. She planned to return to China upon graduation from USC at the end of May 2017, and had been told that a job awaited her return. However, on the day of our appointment, she received notice that the offer of employment had been withdrawn. She was deeply disappointed.

Certainly this news qualified as "adversity," but it fortunately triggered the Sones family motto in me, which I shared with my patient. What followed, in short order, was my suggestion that she develop a business of her own, offering what she had learned at USC to organizations that would not want or need a full-time person providing what she had to offer.

The patient immediately perked up and began to consider possibilities. I reinforced my suggestion with my standard encouragement of patients to "Develop a Business of Your Own" (see Chapter 33, "Develop a Business of Your Own"). Hopefully she would do just that.

40. ADOLESCENT REBELLION

Gary gets very anxious when dealing with anybody he constructs as being in a position of authority; whether that person is someone he works with, a policeman, a doctor, an older person, or what have you. Gary clearly recognizes that the reaction is unreasonable, but he suffers significant discomfort despite that recognition.

Gary is now over forty-three years old, has a successful marriage, is father of two children, has a circle of appreciative friends, and runs a complex business. What's going on here? Why should Gary suffer from severe anxiety when dealing with individuals he sees as "authority" figures?

Like most neurosis, the origins of Gary's difficulties lie in his childhood. His mother was controlling, demanding, and often physically abusive. His father was very passive. Gary never went through an "adolescent rebellion." He finally "rebelled" at the age of forty while he was in treatment with me. It took some two years of no relationship with her, but when he began to reengage with her, he firmly established that she could no longer control him. But the damage had been done. Gary has a program deeply in the structure of the brain that gets activated and gives rise to anxiety whenever he constructs an "authority figure."

Gary may be able to decrease the intensity of his anxiety by a careful exploration of the traumatic childhood experiences with his mother and ideally access and ventilate the associated feelings. But as so often occurs, early childhood trauma gets deeply repressed, and so far he has little access to those memories.

By clearly identifying this anxiety as part of his "child self" and being very clear about its origins, Gary is in process of effecting a separation from that "child self." He is learning to treat that part of self as he would treat a child without: with kindness and understanding, and reassurance that there is now an adult self that is in charge and that will not permit abusive treatment. However, that adult self also must set appropriate and firm limits on that anxious "child self" and not permit it to interfere with adult matters.

Gary's task as outlined above is not easy, but he is moving steadily in the necessary directions.

Gary's case illustrates the clear necessity of the "adolescent rebellion" against an abusive parent. Ideally the child identifies that they are no longer so totally dependent on the parent; this usually occurs in adolescence. They then make it clear to the parent that abusive treatment will no longer be tolerated. Gary's failure to effect an "adolescent rebellion" probably has something to do with the passivity of his father. His father failed to "stand up" to his mother, and Gary probably identified with his father.

Ideally the adolescent has the kind of parents that do not require "rebellion." But, as Gary illustrates, failure to rebel against an abusive parent can result in long-standing painful symptoms.

41. POTENTIAL UNFULFILLED

Delia started therapy with me when she was sixteen years old. Very unusual for an adolescent, she came on her own accord. When I discovered that she was experimenting with heroin, I arranged for a forced hospitalization. After her initial protests settled down, that hospitalization proved to be a turning point in that her lifestyle was no longer characterized by chaos. With many interruptions for varying periods of time, I have continued to see her once a week for some forty-five years.

That "once a week" schedule is a consequence of a very frustrating experience I had with Delia's father. When Delia was ready for discharge from the hospital, I told him that she should continue to be seen several times a week, as she clearly had complex problems that required intensive therapy. And she had clearly shown, during her hospitalization, a capacity to benefit from therapy. Despite his very significant wealth, he refused to support more than once a week. Why he refused was never clear. For a long time, I suspected he thought I was trying to exploit the situation to make money. My patient says he saw her as simply a "rebellious child." I have come to agree with her; he did not recognize the complexity of her problems. Part of that complexity was his deficient role as a parent. I suspect if he did recognize his role, it would have stimulated a great deal of guilt, and he unconsciously resolved that problem by simply seeing her as a "rebellious child."

The reason I found my experience with Delia's father so "frustrating" is that I have long held the belief that Delia could have had a much more fulfilling life if she had the appropriate intensive treatment early on. Over the years, she was subject to periodic depressions. Medication has been helpful, and she has not had a significant depression in several years now. She does have a long-standing relationship with a good man, and it's not that her current life does not have its gratifications. But she never developed a profession, she never had a deeply fulfilling love and sexual life, she never married, and she never had children. Simply put, Delia did not come close to fulfilling her real potential, something I believe she could have done had she had the appropriate intensive therapy early on.

Delia wanted that intensive therapy. As mentioned, early on she did something that adolescents, in my experience, rarely do: she initiated contact with a psychotherapist. During her hospitalization, she clearly demonstrated her ability to benefit from intensive psychotherapy. There was no lack of funds, but her father refused to make them available for the intensive therapy she required. Frustrating!!

So, we've made do with that once-a-week regime over the years. Recently we have been working on her identification with her father and her rejection of her child self.

And most recently she has rediscovered an interest in higher mathematics -- this in a woman who always doubted her intelligence. That doubt was a legacy of her poor school performance before her hospitalization.

42. WHAT TO DO IF HE WON'T COMMIT

Most women want a loving, responsive partner, a home, and a family -- as do most men. However, it is not uncommon for women to find themselves in relationships where the male is unwilling to fully commit. I strongly suspect that a consequence of the sexual liberation of women is a significant increase in the number of men unwilling to commit. In times past, the prohibition that women imposed on premarital intercourse probably helped motivate men to commit -- the principle was "no commitment, no sex." That principle probably had evolutionary roots. The female who had a male committed to helping her was more likely to survive, particularly when she was in advanced stages of pregnancy, and the child of that pregnancy was also more likely to survive. With those evolutionary roots no longer a critical factor and women's lib an important cultural force, many men are able to live by the crude "Why buy the cow when you can get the milk for free?"

Playing a significant role in the complex interaction between men and women is the apparent ability for men to be able to have sexual relations without emotional involvement. Witness to this is the existence of prostitution, which is said to be the world's oldest profession. The vast majority of prostitutes are women. The few male prostitutes are primarily responsive to homosexual males. There just is not much of a market for male prostitutes servicing women. In contrast to men, the vast majority of women have little interest in sexual relations unless there is emotional involvement. And with sexual involvement, women experience an intensification of emotional involvement.

The difference between men and women with regard to sexual relations and emotional involvement probably also has evolutionary roots. If the next generation, a potential consequence of heterosexual relations, is to survive, it must have the deep emotional involvement of the mother. That is the case in all mammals. Witness the reaction, for example, of a mother bear if her cub is threatened. Certainly the emotional involvement of the father enhances the probability of survival of the infant. But the child can survive without his emotional involvement if it has a committed mother. The female versus male reaction of emotional involvement and sexual relations probably has something to do with that necessary maternal commitment to the potential offspring.

Though I have drawn sharp lines between men and women regarding the emotional aspect of sexuality, I want to make it clear that men find sexual experience much more gratifying if there is emotional involvement. For the vast majority of men, sex without that emotional involvement becomes an empty, sterile experience.

However, the differences described between male and female sexuality give rise to a painful problem for a number of women: she is more emotionally involved than he is. That emotional involvement leads her to stay in a relationship where he clearly is unwilling to commit. She is hoping he will change and is unwilling to confront reality. Years can pass by and her longings for home and family go unfulfilled. She finally gets around to recognizing that he does not love her the way she wants to be loved. But the years have taken their toll. She is losing her youthful looks and vitality and is becoming less attractive. Finding that desired mate is more difficult -- not a good outcome.

The point of this essay is clear: If after a reasonable period of time in a relationship (six to twelve months?) you find he is unwilling to commit to marriage, GET OUT! Do not waste your youth on him. Hopefully when he detects you are really going to leave, he becomes aware of how valuable you are, pleads with you to stay, and clearly indicates his willingness to commit. If he doesn't, LEAVE! Go through the pain. It will stop. FIND SOMEONE ELSE!

If you are not able to follow the advice in the above paragraph, consider getting some psychotherapy.

43. ONLINE DATING

On February 29, 2016, Pew Research reported that "55% of Americans who are in a marriage or committed relationship say that they met their significant other on line." That seems to me to be an astonishingly high percentage. But there is no question that online dating has taken center stage in our quest for a love relationship. And I strongly urge my patients to use it. They all hate it.

I understand New York City has a very active "bar scene" where singles meet one another. But here in spread-out Los Angeles, the bar scene is nowhere near as active, and the internet is definitely the way to go, despite the attendant frustrations. Those frustrations have primarily to do with the fact that, unless you are very lucky, most individuals you meet will not fit your particular bill.

The advice that I outline now is directed at heterosexual women; other individuals can readily extract from that advice what is applicable to them. I advise patients to treat the search as a job. Find the internet dating sites that best seem to fulfill your requirements. Go through your respondents and contact them online. Do not give them your phone number to avoid the outside possibility that the male respondent is some sort of a nut. After several exchanges on the internet, you call them. After several phone conversations, arrange to meet at a Starbucks or similar venue. Ideally you have more than one such meeting at different Starbucks. Bring your own transportation. Do not commit to other than the cup of coffee, as most of the time you will probably not want to spend an evening with Mr. Notrite. Perhaps set aside one night a week to execute this usually onerous task.

Hopefully you will find Mr. Rite in short order. More likely you will have to keep at it for an extended period of time. But keep at it. He is out there somewhere, and if you persist you will find him. "Once you have found him never let him go" (from the musical *South Pacific* -- listen to it on the internet).

44. USEFULNESS OF NEGATIVE FANTASY

Recently I was dealing with a patient who suffered significant anxiety because of his involvement in negative, low-probability fantasy. He was very resistant to recognizing that was the case. But in our exchange, he pointed out something that I have failed to emphasize. He said his negative fantasies had made very significant contributions to his success in dealing with the complexities of the entertainment industry.

Of course he was absolutely right. His negative fantasies had made a totally critical contribution to his success. It is entirely accurate to say that without those negative fantasies, he would have been a complete failure.

What I have said about this particular patient applies to human beings in general. Our negative fantasies alert us to potential problems. The context in which they evolved was probably life-threatening danger. And though dangers in current life usually are not life threatening, dangers certainly exist, and if not attended to, they can lead to all sorts of difficulty.

However, we have paid an enormous price for this gift from evolution; it has led to "Most men live lives of quiet desperation." And Thoreau could have added "women" to his profound insight (see Chapter 1, "Reality and Fantasy").

45. PROBLEM OF READING OTHER PEOPLE'S MINDS

This problem is a very common one. Just recently, a patient, we'll call him Mike, told me that his partner, we'll call her Mary, was very disappointed when he visited her at her new office and did not bring her coffee: "*You should have known* how disappointed I would be if you did not bring me coffee. All my friends brought me coffee when they visited me in my new office." (How those friends knew she wanted them to bring coffee is a bit of a mystery.) Mike, who happens to be a very pleasant easy-going (probably too much so) guy, felt guilty that he did not know that she wanted him to bring her coffee.

Both Mary and Mike were involved in "nice clear-cut neurosis" (NCCN) -- Mary because she anticipated that Mike should be able to read her mind, and Mike because of his guilt that he could not do so. The plain fact, despite the claims of some, is that we humans do not have the power to read others' minds. Of course, the more familiar we are with an individual, the more we may be able to predict their reactions. However, ideally we clearly recognize that those predictions are fantasies that do not necessarily correspond to reality.

Ideally Mary and Mike recognize that they are involved in NCCN. Mary, if she wants something of Mike, should tell him, "It would be nice when you come to visit my new office if you brought me a cup of coffee." Mike, if Mary expresses disappointment in his inability to read her mind, ideally flatly states, "I wish I had the power to read your mind, but I don't. If there is something you want of me, like a cup of coffee in your new office, you have to tell me."

Couples can save themselves considerable grief if they follow the recommendations outlined in this essay.

46. WHAT IS THE MEANING OF LIFE?

This is an issue that comes up with some frequency in patients that are in extensive psychotherapy. However, it usually doesn't take much therapeutic time because the vast majority of such patients are convinced, as am I, that life is an accident and that human beings are a product of evolution. That being the case, the obvious answer to the question of "What is the meaning of life?" is that "There is no fundamental meaning."

Religions, with decreasing success in the Western world, try to fill that apparent void. What then for those that cannot find life's meaning in religion? Live in a world without meaning? Facing that reality, some become significantly depressed. Suicide?

Ideally, in my view, one takes up the great challenge of life and *creates* a meaningful, fulfilling life. If there is a god somewhere out there this might not be a bad way to go: "Here is the stuff of life. You are a free agent. Let's see what you can do with it."

Usually key elements in that creation are a fulfilling relationship, stimulating work, children, and friends.

Some of the most tragic patients I have seen in my psychiatric practice are individuals, late in life, who are aware that they have not created a fulfilling, meaningful life. They usually will be cognizant of missed opportunities and suffer deep regret. The consequent depressive states are not easy to treat. And concern about the suicidal potential of these individuals is significant.

Besides the usual treatment for depression, the psychiatrist may be very helpful if they can assist such patients to use what life remains to create fulfilling, meaningful experiences. What will be helpful depends on the particular individual and requires careful evaluation in that individual. However, the everlasting possibility of finding a loving partner is one possibility that exists indefinitely. Further, the therapist should emphasize *hope*, no matter what the circumstances.

47. DOING PSYCHOTHERAPY

This is an example of what I actually do in the office. It is from this kind of exchange with patients that this series of essays evolved.

This first session with a new patient begins when I open the door to my waiting room and introduce myself to the patient. The patient, while sitting in the waiting room, has filled out a form giving their name, address, telephone number, insurance data, etc. The patient hands this form to me, and I invite the patient into the office and invite them to be seated at one of two identical and comfortable chairs.

I have a cup of tea or coffee on the table between the two identical chairs and offer the patient coffee, tea, or water. I review the form to make certain that it is readable and complete, and then go on to inform the patient that I do not speak to anybody about the patient without the patient's specific permission. I then go on to explain that the government now requires that we give the patient a copy of the rules regarding patient privacy (HIPAA), and I have the patient sign a form acknowledging receipt of a copy of those rules.

I ask the patient if it is okay to take notes. (I've never had a patient that refused permission.)

I then ask if the patient has ever seen a psychiatrist or psychotherapist. If the patient responds affirmatively, then I investigate what occurred in previous encounters with special attention to prior use of psychiatric drugs. If the patient has never seen a therapist (which is getting increasingly unusual), I then ask how the patient felt about coming in. The usual response is to acknowledge some anxiety. I then go on to say that this is the usual reaction, "but it is surprising how rapidly people get over that anxiety. Perhaps it is easier to sit down and talk about these intimate matters with a total stranger."

Next I say, "Take it wherever you want to go. If you wish, ask me questions, or if you prefer, I can ask you questions. Or you can begin by telling me what led you to come in at this time. However you want to proceed."

Usually the patient begins by telling me what brought them in. (I will go on now with a specific example.) She, we'll call her Maria, starts to tell me that her boyfriend, we'll call him Dick, has dumped her. She immediately begins to cry with some intensity and tells me that she has not been able to stop crying. I ask how long she had been with him. She replies, "A year and a half." I respond by reassuring her that it is normal to cry after this kind of experience, that her tears are indicative of her capacity to love someone, and that they will stop over time. I also tell her that talking and crying about the experience with a therapist might help accelerate getting over it. She seems reassured and her crying decreases a bit.

Maria then goes on to tell me that he had been treating her harshly for some time, but she clearly states that she could not identify anything she had done to warrant the harsh treatment. She goes on with apparent pain to state, "I guess I just wasn't good enough." And this is followed by a return to crying with some intensity.

Now this last paragraph is what, ideally, the therapist is particularly listening for. In contrast to "normal" tears consequent to the loss of a love relationship, they are what I label as "nice clear-cut neurosis" (NCCN). To amplify on that term a bit, one has to leave plenty of room for "normal" reactions. If there is a question as to whether the reaction is or is not normal, in general it is best to leave it and to stay tuned for NCCN, for it is in dealing with NCCN that the therapist is most likely to make a significant contribution to the patient being freer of pain and living a more fulfilling life.

Maria's statement that he had been treating her harshly for some time qualifies as an NCCN because if you were not neurotic, you would not stay in such a relationship. Further, her conclusion that he treats her harshly because "I just wasn't good enough" is without justification. If he felt she wasn't "good enough," he would have simply terminated the relationship early on rather than waiting one and a half years and treating her harshly.

I point out the NCCN to Maria and seek her agreement that these are indeed instances of NCCN. If Maria were to disagree that this was NCCN, a debate would follow. One very frequently effective way of getting patients to recognize the existence of NCCN is to ask the patient how they would react if someone was telling them this story. That method frequently is effective as it helps separate them from their personal reactivity.

If Maria were to insist her reactions were not NCCN, the therapist would do well to resign to Maria being a very difficult case and would move on and hope for future opportunities. However, Maria, as is near invariably the case, agrees with me. It is apparent to Maria that she should have left Dick some time ago. Further, Maria recognizes that her tendency to see herself as "not good enough" is a long-standing NCCN that plays a central role in her permitting Dick's abuse. I reinforce Maria's insight by emphasizing that self-esteem can never be dependent on assessment by another, as who knows what the problems of the other are; Dick probably had deep neurotic needs to attack her self-esteem, probably in an unsuccessful effort to elevate his own.

Once an NCCN is *identified*, I strongly suggest that she resign to its presence. I tell her that this neurotic reactivity is deeply programmed in the neuronal structure of the brain, and there is no delete button. *Resignation* can help Maria be alert to when an NCCN is active and she can then employ techniques to deal with the NCCN.

I tell Maria that one technique that may immediately assist in dealing with an NCCN is the deliberate *turning of attention away* from the NCCN to ongoing reality (see Chapter 3, "Training Attention"). I reinforce how difficult it is to implement this suggestion, that it requires a great deal of practice but can be a significant help.

I then go on to suggest that an NCCN usually is a traumatic legacy of one's childhood and that in dealing with NCCN it is frequently helpful to attempt to deal with this legacy by identifying it as part of the "child within." I then go on to say that everyone has a "child within." Nobody has the perfect childhood, the perfect parents, etc. There is always some "screwed up" programming that gets into the brain and that gives rise to NCCN. And sadly, there is no delete button, but there are some techniques available to lessen the pain it causes. Identifying the NCCN as part of the "child within" is another one of those techniques as it helps to separate the NCCN from the healthy, non-neurotic, reality-testing "adult self." The adult self can then go on to an analysis of this NCCN, this legacy of childhood.

Ideally one treats the disturbed "child within" the way one would treat a disturbed "child without." That is, the child is accepted with warmth and an attempt to understand what the problem is. In Maria's case, she had alcoholic parents that frequently treated her harshly (see Chapter 16, "Feelings of Inferiority"). Maria, as a youngster totally dependent on her parents, was unable to recognize her parents' clear problems. She needed them to be paragons of strength and wisdom. If there were problems in their relationship, it must be she that was the defective one, hence lifelong feelings of inferiority.

I then assist Maria in recognizing that her child self was clearly "running the show" in her relationship with Dick. I strongly suggest that though that child self is dealt with warmly, it cannot be permitted to control behavior. To the extent it does so, to that extent she will be subject to feelings of inferiority, which are a major pathway to significant depressions.

The intellectual recognition of the problem by the adult self helps to effect the further separation of the adult self from the child self. I reinforce the need to resign to the presence of feelings of "not being good enough" as resignation will help her stay alert if those feelings get activated. I suggest that though they will never leave completely, she may be able to decrease the intensity of these feelings by attempting in the therapeutic situation to relive those painful experiences with parents. The attempt is to activate those old feelings and discharge them to the extent possible.

Activating those old experiences and their associated feelings is not easy, but ideally the patient makes that attempt. One can look at this attempt as an effort to give the child within an opportunity to express its unhappiness to the loving, accepting adult self. If successful, the child self is less intrusive into the adult world and the adult self becomes the appropriately dominant self, a self that will not tolerate abusive treatment and has a solid, healthy self-esteem.

48. WAR

For some time I have been considering writing about war. Usually after some thinking about it, I would give it up. I finally decided to write about it as a clear example of NCCN (nice clear-cut neurosis).

What are we doing? Killing and maiming one another? Storing weapons that with a single blow can annihilate hundreds of thousands of our fellow human beings? Running the risk that we and our loved ones join the dead or injured? What in God's name are we doing? Clearly this is NCCN on a massively destructive scale.

How did we get here? Why do we continue? I suspect that old evolutionary drives are operative. It well could have been that back in times long past, if you did not occupy some of the limited amount of land that contained a food supply, such as fruit trees, you would not survive. Survival was favored by the development of very aggressive individuals who would protect the group's territory and seek to extend it. And the populous appreciated, romanced, and applauded their aggressiveness.

A very interesting offshoot of war: it may have driven evolutionary forces that led to our becoming the dominant creature in the world. That group that produced individuals that created the best, most effective weapons would be most likely to survive. And some of our best brains continue to develop better and better weapons.

Conditions that existed in those times long past no longer exist. The world is now occupied by nation-states, and land is generally available to feed the populous. Even if land is not available, arrangements can be made to import what the populous requires.

Peaceful, cooperative individuals are the overwhelming majority of humans. Perhaps they too operate out of old evolutionary drives. They passively cooperate with aggressive leaders and will join in to kill fellow humans.

Solutions to this massively destructive NCCN are not readily available, but they obviously must be found. Perhaps framing it as an NCCN and turning our most effective brains to finding solutions will help.

P.S. Consider what you could do if the money spent on armaments was instead used to better conditions for human beings.

49. FINAL ESSAY

On occasion, in the course of my work, I have had an opportunity to see three generations of a family. Strikingly, all suffer from the same neurotic problems. And I suspect that were earlier generations available, many of them would also suffer from the same neurotic problems. Though some, for a variety of reasons, may not be affected, such as a caretaker that has marked influence.

Each generation has a responsibility to be as free of neurosis as possible. This is mandatory, as neurotic problems in one generation are near inevitably passed on to the next generation.

Hopefully what I have written in this book will help your generation rid itself of neurosis.

Made in the USA
Las Vegas, NV
05 February 2022

42992969R10075